QUICK & EASY

CONTAINER WATER GARDENS

QUICK & EASY

CONTAINER
WATER GARDENS

Simple-to-Make Water Features and
Fountains for Indoor and Outdoor Gardens

PHILIP SWINDELLS

STOREY

Storey Books
Schoolhouse Road
Pownal, Vermont 05261

Copyright © 1998 Quarto Inc.

United States edition published in 1998 by Storey Books,
Schoolhouse Road, Pownal,
Vermont 05261.

The mission of Storey Communications is to serve our customers
by publishing practical information that encourages personal
independence in harmony with the environment.

This book was designed and produced by
Quarto Publishing plc
The Old Brewery
6 Blundell Street
London N7 9BH

Editor Ulla Weinberg
Art editors Elizabeth Healey, Suzanne Metcalfe-Megginson
Copy editors Mary Flower, Gwen Rigby
Designer Vicki James
Photographers Ian Howes, Jon Wyand
Illustrator John Woodcock
Picture researchers Gill Metcalfe, Christine Lalla
Art director Moira Clinch
Assistant art director Penny Cobb
Storey Books editor Gwen W. Steege
QUAR.CWG

Manufactured in China by Regent Publishing Services Ltd.
Printed in China by Leefung Asco Printers Ltd.

10 9 8 7 6 5 4

Library of Congress Cataloging-in-Publication Data
Available on request

ISBN 1-58017-080-3

Contents

❧

OFTEN A WATER FEATURE forms the central focal point in a garden, and is surrounded by planters spilling over with colorful plants, or perhaps with subtle-colored foliage in interesting shapes.

Primula beesiana

Introduction

❧

Water is one of the most fascinating elements in the garden. Whether it is a still pond that reflects all around it, or a gentle whispering fountain, it holds a fascination for old and young alike. Water gardening is no longer the prerogative of those with large gardens and generous bank accounts, but a pleasure that can be enjoyed and afforded by all.

The introduction of new materials, such as Ethylene-Propylene-Diene-Monomer (EPDM) and fiberglass for pool construction, has revolutionized water gardening. Pumps and filters have also become much simpler and smaller over the last few years. Today you don't need large pumps and ugly pump houses to create a fountain or waterfall. Just place a simple, small, powerful submersible pump in the water, and switch it on.

Such innovations mean that smaller units can be successfully created, permitting water features on even the tiniest yard, patio or balcony, often planted with miniature aquatics. Water in the garden or outdoor living space is now truly within everyone's range. Container water gardens are not only fashionable but immensely varied and practical, and as they need relatively little maintenance they are ideal for busy people. They also provide an instant effect that in many cases is portable, although, as with other types of gardening, it always takes time for the plants to grow to maturity.

An outdoor container water garden has limited winter appeal. Unlike more extensive garden pools, which can be arranged to look good even when the plants have died down, container water gardens have insufficient open water surface to make this sort of impact. They are similar to tubs and planters containing flowering plants—a spring- and summer-long pleasure that will often be dismantled and stored away during the winter.

The advantage of a container water feature is its versatility. It can be almost anything you want it to be, from a celebration of moving water to a cameo wildlife pool. If the container is carefully chosen, it can become an integral part of the design. The Dutch, those masters of horticulture, use what they call "mobile gardens," that is, contained features that can be moved around and changed at will. The plants are grown in

inserts, which are lifted and removed from the larger containers as plants pass their best and the display needs changing. They are constantly replaced by fresh inserts with the same plant in prime condition, or a different one to add interest to the garden feature.

Such configurations of containers, and the ability to change them regularly, make mobile gardens something new and exciting, especially for gardeners who have inherited stark, barren courtyards or patios and want a quick way to transform them into attractive garden areas.

Nymphaea 'Aurora'

FISH CAN BE ACCOMMODATED IN MORE SPACIOUS CONTAINERS, but they are generally short-term inhabitants, as few would survive the winter in colder climates in such a small body of water.

BAMBOO CREATIONS vary from dripping water and swinging chutes to organ pipelike upright groups of cane, through which water gushes and bubbles.

Zantedeschia elliottiana

Container water features can be very diverse, ranging from a miniature waterscape to a geyser gushing through a mound of washed pebbles. If a container can hold water, it is a potential water feature. A wide variety of ready-made water features are available from garden centers, and great sophistication can be achieved with a screwdriver and the ability to connect a plug to a power supply, as some of the prefabricated units and combinations are excellent and extremely reliable. If you enjoy creating things, ready-made items may seem less satisfying and the opportunities for making your own unique feature are endless.

Where space is at a premium and moving water is desired, consider the flexibility offered by a self-contained fountain kit. These are usually wall-mounted with a bowl in a unit that incorporates a small pump, and merely requires the addition of water for the desired effect. A whole range of fountains can be used on their own indoors or, with some more elaborate additions, outside. The great advantage of such a modest feature is that it provides moving water for your garden, does not require plants or fish, and is one of the few water features that can be successfully situated in the shade.

There is quite a long history of small water features in the Far East, and Oriental gardens are a rich source of inspiration, especially for ideas for fountains. Millstones with water bubbling through them are an adaptation of a traditional Oriental idea, and bamboo, currently very fashionable in the West, has long been used by the Japanese in water features. The most popular fountain is the traditional deer scarer, or *shishi-odoshi*, which would make an amusing and decorative focal point for any garden.

Introduction **9**

Planning and Design

Although container water features are quite small, they still need to be carefully planned if they are to be a practical and visual success. Their position within a garden is also important. Although the water feature itself may be tastefully planted, it is crucial that, as an element of the garden landscape, it fits into the overall design. This is particularly relevant where the container feature is not easily movable or is sunk into the ground.

BE SPARING IN YOUR PLANTING Allow the water surface itself to play a part in the water feature.

The first thing to realize is that a container water garden is rarely self-sustaining, and it is almost impossible to create a natural balance within such a feature. This means that when planting it you have to keep in mind that it will need to be periodically emptied. Therefore, both the position of the feature itself and the planting arrangements must be carefully considered.

Irrespective of the type of water feature, it should be situated in full sun, as most plants suitable for water gardening require sunlight to thrive. There is little to be gained by positioning water out of the sun—a dancing fountain in the shade does not have much visual impact.

Otherwise, the way in which you introduce water into your garden is very much a matter of personal taste. Small pools and tubs are at their most attractive when

A SELF-CONTAINED water feature with peripheral planting.

viewed at close quarters, so it makes sense to site them close to areas where people sit and relax. Where moving water is involved, especially a fountain, make sure that the site is sheltered. Wind and fitful breezes cause the spray from a fountain to blow around, making it uncomfortable for anyone to sit or garden in the vicinity. It also creates more work, as the reservoir has to be constantly refilled to prevent the pump from running dry and overheating.

A rarely considered advantage of container water gardening is that it provides an opportunity for plant enthusiasts to grow unusual varieties that would not flourish in the rest of the garden. A watertight window box, solidly planted with bog garden plants and watered heavily, produces a spectacle of fascinating and colorful plants that could otherwise only be enjoyed in a custom-made bog garden.

Most gardeners prefer outdoor features as they are much easier to control and manage, especially where plants are involved. With indoor features and in warmer climates, you can use tropical plants. Choose varieties that are small and undemanding, as many tropical plants are tall and occupy a lot of space. When arranging the planting within a container, remember that water is important for its own sake. Do not plant so that the water is entirely lost to view, unless, of course, you intend to make a bog garden.

Where plants are meant to be an integral part of a feature, they must be taken into account from the outset. In order to thrive most of them must be placed in a sunny position. While some of the submerged, weedy aquatics exist with their roots in gravel, all others, except those that float on the surface, must have their roots in aquatic potting mix. Some will flourish in a modest amount of potting mix, but you must treat others in the same way you would if you planned to grow them in a

conventional pond: provide them with fair-sized planting baskets and adequate amounts of potting mix.

If you find it difficult to plant up the part of the feature that contains water, consider the possibility of peripheral planting. It is often simpler to create the water part of your design as you want it, and then place this in another watertight container in which plants can be grown in an accompanying role. Such plantings often produce a more harmonious, less contrived effect.

While everyone enjoys having fish in a water feature, great caution

BRIGHT LIGHT creates much of the attraction of water in the garden, especially when it is moving.

Hosta fortunei 'Gold Standard'

should be exercised when introducing them into sinks and pots. Fish require a generous water surface to provide them with sufficient oxygen, and a reasonable depth of water in order to keep cool. Only large commercial barrels or self-built constructions are likely to be deep enough and, more important, have sufficient water surface area to accomodate fish safely. They can be kept where there is continuous turbulent water, as this provides a ready supply of oxygen, but it is hardly fair to keep any creature in endless frothing and foaming water.

Iris versicolor

Unplanted water features, which provide the soothing sound and visual pleasure of water, are often a good idea and are particularly easy to care for, as they require almost no maintenance. Where the water is the main element of the feature and plants do not figure, take into consideration stillness, reflection, movement, color, and sound. Water can bring all these qualities to a garden if you plan the feature thoughtfully. The manner in which you achieve this can be almost as varied as the features themselves, ranging from drips and gushes to trickles and sprays. Moving water can differ widely in its effect, not only with regard to sound but also to light: both overcast skies or contrasting bright sunshine can play an important part. So when planning and designing your water feature, take all of these aspects into account.

Making made easy

So many different containers can be used, adapted, or created to produce a container water feature—the only limits are your imagination and creative skills. Where plants and fish are involved, there are a few constraints, but otherwise, provided the construction functions properly, anything will work.

When you have decided on the kind of water feature you want, and have considered the questions of plants and fish, you can turn your

IF A CONTAINER WILL HOLD WATER, or can be made to hold water, it can be turned into a small water feature. The type and arrangement of the plants determine whether you create a traditional or unusual effect.

attention to cost. Some ready-made features are expensive for what they are, but others provide excellent value and are very attractive, particularly when dressed and surrounded by plants of your choice. With small alterations and adaptations many containers intended for a totally different purpose can be used for container water gardening. For example, you can plug the drainage holes in large ceramic and terra-cotta pots meant for garden plants with fine aggregate concrete, and waterproof them successfully with transparent sealant. Some specialist water gardening centers will do this for you if you don't feel confident doing it yourself. Likewise you can drill pots and rocks to take a small waterfall or fountain outlet; again, many aquatics specialists will be happy to do this for you.

While most water features are created in waterproof containers, you should not overlook the possibility of using a pool liner to line any object that is not watertight. There are many different kinds of liner, but the toughest and easiest to mold into a shape without awkward creases are made from EPDM. This can be purchased off the roll, and you can buy just as much as you need. Polyethylene liners, although much cheaper, have a limited life.

Making a container water feature can be quite simple and, for the budget-conscious, very economical, as you can use all kinds of

DECORATIVE TUB GARDENS offer a low-maintenance water garden option.

Matteuccia struthiopteris

ingenious devices. However, the one area where economy should not rule is in purchasing a pump. Go for the best value by all means, but be sure that the pump is reliable and will carry out the task that you set it.

Once installed, and providing it is properly constructed, a water feature is one of the easiest and most pleasurable garden features to maintain. I hope the suggestions in this book will inspire and encourage you to create a small oasis in your own garden or yard.

Calm Elegance

A pond with still water adds a unique
quality to gardens and patios of any size.
Its surface reflects the movements of the
sky and everything around it; and even
when confined to a small container, water
can bring peace and tranquility to a garden.
Many aquatic plants prefer the conditions in
still water, so you can create a lush feature
with marginal and bog plants.

Raise the Barrel

>❦

You can create a lovely water garden in a barrel or cask. The barrel must have a consistent water level and not be in use for collecting water—it has to be a feature in its own right.

YOU WILL NEED

- Barrel or cask
- Stone or hardcore
- Pea gravel
- Bricks
- Planting containers
- Aquatic potting mix

PLANTING

① *Ceratophyllum demersum* (submerged)
② *Veronica beccabunga*
③ *Myriophyllum aquaticum* (submerged)
④ *Iris laevigata* 'Rose Queen'
⑤ *Nymphaea* 'Aurora'
⑥ *Lysimachia nummularia* 'Aurea'

Barrels and casks may present problems with water levels, as few aquatic plants will tolerate over 3 feet (1m) of water. There are two ways to deal with this. The best is to raise the base level within the barrel with a solid material, which can be stone or anything else that is bulky and will not pollute the water. Top this off with fine gravel to produce a level surface. This provides stability for the barrel and allows you to arrange plants more easily, while from the outside the visual effect is maintained.

If you want to retain the full depth of water in a wooden barrel you can do this by screwing shelves to the inside, or you can use crosspieces fastened inside the barrel to support the plants. The latter is also possible with a plastic cask. The problems of maintaining such a feature are, however, compounded by the fact that the water is so deep, and that any debris falling to the bottom can only be removed by completely dismantling the feature. If the barrel is only a third full of water, it can be treated in the same way as any other small pond.

The barrel featured here has been planted with a waterlily, *Nymphaea* 'Aurora', as a centerpiece, and *Iris laevigata* 'Rose Queen' and *Veronica beccabunga* to dress the edges. The waterlily is grown in a container filled with aquatic potting mix in the deeper part of the barrel, so that it is covered by no more than 20 inches (50cm) of water. The marginal plants are grown in aquatic potting mix in baskets raised on bricks so that they are just beneath the water surface. Parrot feather and hornwort, *Myriophyllum aquaticum* and *Ceratophyllum demersum*, provide submerged aquatic plant growth.

Lowering the Level

Constructed of natural material, a sunken barrel pond fits easily into a more rustic garden setting, becoming part of the localized landscape rather than being imposed upon it.

YOU WILL NEED

- Half-barrel
- Pool liner or transparent sealant
- Water-soluble wood preservative
- Small latticework aquatic planter
- Aquatic potting mix
- Discarded pantyhose
- Bricks or stones

A sunken barrel pond is especially suitable for colder climates. Water is less likely to freeze in the ground, and in most cases hardy aquatic plants, and even small common goldfish, will overwinter without difficulty in such a feature.

Most sunken barrels are made of wood with metal straps, although there are also some convincing solid plastic kinds available. Wooden barrel pools are generally made from half a barrel of the type that contained a liquid, usually whiskey or beer. There are some cheaper ones about that have been used for tar or oil products, but these should be avoided. It is best to purchase a new barrel from a garden center and either seal it with a transparent sealant inside, or line it with black pool liner.

When preparing to sink the barrel into the ground, dig the hole to a depth that allows about 4 inches (10cm) of the barrel to protrude above soil level. The effect is much better when the edge is exposed, and the raised edge also prevents inquisitive small animals such as mice from falling in if they arrive to take a drink. While most barrels sold in garden centers are sufficiently well preserved for general garden use, sinking them into the ground does hasten their demise. So it is advisable to paint preservative on the outside or to tack plastic pool liner to the sides to keep the wood dry. Make sure the liner is a good fit, as any water trapped between it and the barrel can cause rotting.

Planting a barrel is simple. Choose a single waterlily, such as *Nymphaea* 'Aurora' or *N. tetragona* 'Helvola', as a centerpiece, and grow it in a small latticework aquatic planter. Although the marginal plants, *Typha minima* and *Iris laevigata* can be planted on the floor of the barrel directly into aquatic potting mix, there will be no control over their growth or the water depth over their crowns. They should rather be grown in small bags created from old pantyhose and raised to the desired level on bricks or stones set close to the side of the barrel. Add *Mimulus x hybridus* 'Calypso', or alternatively *M. ringens*, for a dash of color outside the barrel.

PLANTING

① *Iris laevigata*
② *Nymphaea tetragona* 'Helvola'
③ *Typha minima*
④ *Mimulus x hybridus* 'Calypso'

In the Sink

Old sinks make wonderful water features. Although the whiteness of the traditional kitchen can be too stark for some locations, if tastefully planted the plain white of the container can provide a happy contrast.

YOU WILL NEED

- Old kitchen sink
- Cement and sand mix or plug
- Sealant
- Stones or bricks
- Pieces of rock
- Aquatic potting mix and sand
- Planting containers

The sink should be positioned in a part of the garden where other plantings can provide a fresh green background. Standing alone on a terrace or patio, it can look a little stark.

Seal the drainage hole, either by inserting a plug, or by blocking it up with a fine concrete mix and then painting on a sealant. For the best effect raise the sink on stones or bricks. Not only does this allow for drainage if it leaks around the plug hole, but it also presents the feature better and puts it at a comfortable height for easy maintenance.

The design and planting of the sink should be simple if it is to be effective. One or two pieces of rock positioned so that they appear just above the water level is ideal. The gaps between the edges of the rocks can then be filled with aquatic potting mix to allow for marginal planting. When choosing rocks for a miniature waterscape, avoid sandstone or limestone as they often crumble when immersed in water.

If you wanted water to be an integral visual part of this design, planting would need to be very sparse indeed and the hard lines and color of the sink would dominate the feature. It is therefore better to choose a lush, but not overcrowded planting scheme. Most of the water surface in this feature is occupied by a pygmy red waterlily, *Nymphaea tetragona* 'Rubra', and the floating foliage of the water chestnut, *Trapa natans*. *Eleocharis acicularis* is grown as a submerged plant and the white marsh marigold, *Caltha palustris* 'Alba', and *Typha minima* as marginal plants.

The eleocharis should be encouraged to carpet the floor of the sink with its fine grassy foliage. Place a thin layer of aquatic potting mix mixed with sand on the bottom of the sink and plant small groups of the plant into it. The eleocharis should then spread like an underwater lawn. Grow the waterlily in a very small container, such as a latticework pot cover, placed in the center of the sink, and allow the water chestnut to float about freely.

PLANTING

1. *Nymphaea tetragona* 'Rubra'
2. *Trapa natans*
3. *Eleocharis acicularis* (submerged)
4. *Caltha palustris* 'Alba'
5. *Typha minima*

Eastern Tranquility

This water feature takes its character from the Orient. It could stand on its own, or be a focal point in a more extensive Oriental setting. The planting is representative of the Japanese style.

YOU WILL NEED

- Rectangular bamboo container
- Pool liner
- Square plastic container
- Small, open latticework container
- Aquatic potting mix
- Lime-free potting mix
- Stones or bricks
- Pieces of rock

PLANTING

① *Iris ensata* 'Queen of the Blues'
② Moss
③ *Typha minima*

Bamboo containers of this type are widely sold as planters for indoor plants or summer annuals on the patio or terrace. Some have plastic or metal inserts to protect the wooden interior. While this is satisfactory for ordinary garden plants, it is not a reliable protection in a water feature. Be sure that any bamboo container you buy can be lined with pool liner to make it watertight. This means the planter should have some timber or plywood inside to which the liner can be fastened, as it is quite difficult to secure a pool liner to bamboo.

Within the lined planter, place a large plastic pot, preferably a square one without drainage holes, so that you can isolate an area free from water to represent land. Pack potting mix in and around this pot to give it a fixed position. It is not necessary to use aquatic potting mix for this, but as the acid-loving *Iris ensata* is the main focal plant you should use a lime-free potting mix. The dwarf Japanese reedmace, *Typha minima*, is grown in a small, open latticework container filled with aquatic potting mix. Place the container into the water, and raise it on a brick or stone if necessary to bring it to within about 2 inches (5cm) of the water surface.

Level off the potting mix in the container representing the land, and carefully place two rocks on top of it to give the feature the character of a miniature landscape. Avoid rocks that contain calcium, such as limestone; instead choose hard rocks, ideally granite or slate. If they are well-weathered, all the better.

If the feature is to stand in a cool, damp, and partially shaded position, the natural look can be enhanced by introducing moss into it. Take pieces of suitable moss with a thin layer of soil and position them as close together as possible on the surface of the potting mix between the rocks. They should then quickly unite.

Matching Set

❧

This project provides an opportunity to mix and match a water feature to suit your circumstances. It can be moved around the patio or garden like furniture, just like a Dutch "mobile garden."

YOU WILL NEED

The sizes of the three containers are: 36 x 24 inches (90 x 60cm), 24 x 18 inches (60 x 45cm), and 18 x 12 inches (45 x 30cm).

Cut from ½in (12.5mm) exterior plywood:
- Two 36 x 16in (90 x 40cm); two 24 x 16in (60 x 40cm); one 24 x 35in (60 x 88cm)
- Two 24 x 14in (60 x 35cm); two 18 x 14in (45 x 35cm); one 23 x 18in (58 x 45cm)
- Two 18 x 12in (45 x 30cm); two 12 x 12in (30 x 30cm); one 17 x 12in (43 x 30cm)

- 18–20 thin round fence posts, split in half
- 48 plastic corner joints
- ½in (12.5mm) screws
- 5in (12.5cm) nails
- Brads
- Pool liner
- Hammer, staple gun, saw, screwdriver, drill
- Water-soluble wood preservative
- Aquatic potting mix
- Bricks or inverted planting baskets
- Planting baskets
- Pea gravel

◁ **ONE**

Place the base board on a flat surface and, making sure the box is square, tack the sides together with brads.

▽ **TWO**

Secure the top corners of the box with eight plastic corner joints. This will give the box rigidity.

△ **THREE**

Drop the base out of the box and turn it upside down.

▽ **FOUR**

Screw in eight more corner joints, this time on the sides and positioned about 3 inches (7.5cm) from each corner. These provide support for the base and keep it off the ground and therefore free from damp. Drop the base back into the frame. Paint with wood preservative.

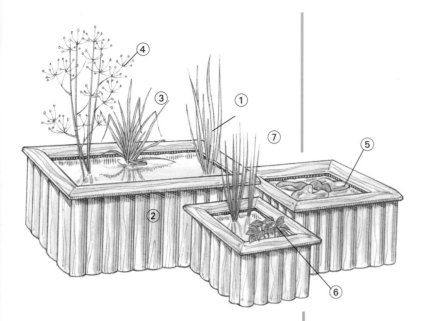

Saw the fence posts to length. As fence posts vary in thickness, try them against the box before screwing them in position.

SIX ▷

Overlap the lengths of fence post at the corners to ensure that they fit snugly.

THE PLANTS USED

This group of containers offers many opportunities for planting a wide range of aquatics, provided that the water remains still. Although water flowing among them would not benefit the plants, it would be an added attraction.

(1) *Acorus calamus* 'Variegatus'
(2) *Myriophyllum aquaticum* (submerged)
(3) *Carex elata* 'Bowles' Golden'
(4) *Alisma plantago-aquatica*
(5) *Nymphaea* 'Aurora'
(6) *Houttuynia cordata* 'Chameleon'
(7) *Typha minima*

◁ **SEVEN**

From the remaining fence posts, cut capping logs to size, with their corners cut to 45-degree-angle miters. Paint them with wood preservative.

△ EIGHT

Install the liner and fasten it at the top with staples before fixing the capping. To avoid splitting the capping, drill pilot holes through and hammer in the nails at an angle, pointing toward the middle. This will lock the top in place.

▽ TEN

Plant aquatics in planting baskets, using aquatic planting mix. Top-dress the baskets with a generous layer of pea gravel to prevent the planting mix from clouding the water.

△ ELEVEN

Plant the waterlily in an aquatic planting basket and place it in position before adding water to the container.

△ NINE

The containers are now ready for planting. In order to bring the plants to the correct level, raise them on inverted planting baskets or bricks.

TWELVE ▷

Soak the freshly planted aquatics with water before putting them in position. This drives out the air and prevents the planting mix from bubbling and escaping into the water when it is added to the containers.

Purely Plants

❧

Traditional terra-cotta pots in varying shapes and sizes can be planted with aquatic plants and arranged to great effect on a paved terrace or patio, or alternatively on a pebble bed.

YOU WILL NEED

- Three soft-colored terra-cotta pots in different sizes and shapes
- Pea gravel
- Aquatic potting mix

PLANTING

1. *Butomus umbellatus*
2. *Iris laevigata* 'Rose Queen'
3. *Juncus effusus* 'Spiralis'
4. *Lysimachia nummularia*
5. *Lysimachia nummularia* 'Aurea'
6. *Pontederia cordata*
7. *Sagittaria sagittifolia* 'Flore Pleno'
8. *Iris laevigata* 'Variegata'
9. *Iris laevigata* 'Colchesteri'

Where you position the three containers depends on the effect sought, whether one of focus and contrast, or of soft harmony. On a hard, reflective surface the design and look of the pots are very important, but in association with other plantings they are more a means to an end.

Most terra-cotta pots are suitable for this kind of water feature. Because the volume of water they contain is relatively small, it will freeze quickly, and you will need to bring them indoors during the winter in colder areas. It is therefore possible to use some fine, fancy designs that are not frost resistant. In winter, drain off the water, but leave the plants growing in the pots and place them in a frost-free, but cool, place. They will come to no harm and can be started into growth again the following spring.

For the best effect you should treat the pots as if they were miniature swamps. Fill the containers at least two-thirds full with aquatic potting mix, plant them up, top them off with pea gravel, and then add water. The plants should not stand in more than 6 inches (15cm) of water. There is a potential problem with mosquitoes with this type of feature, as the water is deep enough for their larvae to survive and yet not deep enough to house fish to eat them. You can solve this problem by adding a drop of cooking oil to the water every couple of weeks. It creates a film over the water surface that is harmless to plants but prevents mosquito larvae coming up for air. In this feature, the appearance of the water surface is not important, since it is rarely visible as the pots become completely filled with plants.

In your planting arrangement, keep away from vigorous, tall plants, which may unbalance the containers both visually and literally in a high wind. Use creeping plants such as the golden-leafed *Lysimachia nummularia* 'Aurea' to provide tumbling foliage over the edge. Other marginal plants in this feature include *Butomus umbellatus*, varieties of *Iris laevigata*, *Pontederia cordata*, and *Juncus effusus* 'Spiralis'. Do not choose more than two or three upright-growing plants for each container if they are to live happily together.

On the Shelf

❧

A delightful miniature water garden can be created in a window box. For the best effect, think carefully about its position and planting scheme.

YOU WILL NEED
- Window box insert or plastic trough
- Aquatic potting mix
- Latticework plant-pot holders or covers, or other planting containers

PLANTING
1. *Lysimachia nummularia* 'Aurea'
2. *Mimulus x hybridus* 'Calypso'
3. *Mimulus x hybridus* 'Queen's Prize'
4. *Primula vialii*
5. *Sisyrinchium angustifolium*

A successful water feature can be created in a window box, but remember that the weight of saturated potting mix and water is considerable, and so the box cannot be situated in the conventional position with the usual brackets. If you want the feature next to your window, it must be positioned on a solid window ledge. The disadvantage of this may be that the plants might grow taller than desired and obscure the view.

While this water feature does not necessarily have standing water in it, the soil must be saturated, and so a watertight container is required. There are many troughs and window box inserts to choose from. Generally troughs have no drainage holes and are perfect for the job; the inserts that fit into traditional window boxes mostly have drainage holes that have to be blocked and made reliably watertight.

Bog garden plants are most suitable for this kind of container. They can be planted either directly into the potting mix in the box, or placed side by side in small latticework pots. Plant-pot holders or covers often serve this purpose well, as they have open sides and are available in sizes that fit readily into a window box. Most proper aquatic planting baskets are too large. Although a solidly planted feature may look slightly more natural, plants growing side by side in pots are isolated from one another and are easier to control, since their roots will not grow together. They can also be easily lifted out for division or replacement. Select fibrous-rooted plants rather than those that produce creeping underground stems or rhizomes, as they are much better behaved and reduce to a minimum the need for control.

Mimulus and primulas are excellent for such features *Mimulus x hybridus* 'Calypso' and *M.* 'Queen's Prize' provide summer-long color, and *Sisyrinchium angustifolium* a variation in stature and habit. *Primula vialii* produces startling lilac and red flowers in late spring before the mimulus start blooming. Although perennials, in a window box they are best treated as annuals and replaced regularly, thereby ensuring a fresh, colorful, and long-lasting display.

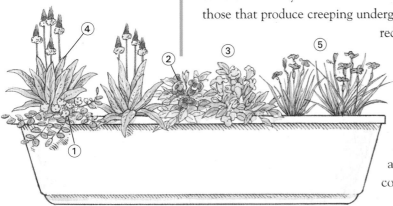

Watering!

❧

The possibilities for creating interesting small water gardens are endless. Here, a good-looking metal watering can is used as the starting point for an attractive feature.

YOU WILL NEED

- Metal watering can
- Aquatic potting mix

Any container that holds water can be used to make a water feature, and one of the most common objects in the garden is the watering can. Planted up it can be a most attractive water garden feature.

By situating it on a paved or gravel base, as if it were simply standing out in the garden, but in a position where it is a focal point and surrounded by a mixed planting, it will appear a natural part of the garden scene, just as planted wheelbarrows do. For the small garden or yard with limited space a single watering can works best, but when you have a little more room, two cans of different shapes and sizes can be used to complement one another.

It is possible to use a watering can as the outlet for a pump, the water filling the can and spraying from the spout. However, quite a powerful pump is required to lift the water sufficiently to make it spray rather than dribble. It can be done, but it is more successful as a feature in association with a larger pool setting.

A wide range of plants will adapt to the growing conditions in a watering can, which can be equated with those of the pool margin or bog garden, depending on how much water is added. Visually, a long, low can works best with frothing, tumbling plants, such as *Veronica beccabunga* and *Lysimachia nummularia* 'Aurea', growing out of the top and spilling over. An upright can will take taller plants better. Choose an elegant marginal, such as the rushlike pink-flowered *Butomus umbellatus*, as a focal point.

Use aquatic potting mix as the growing medium and fill the watering can halfway. Do not plant anything inside until the foliage is tall enough to come above the rim. The emerging plants will be weak if you plant them initially in the gloom of the watering can's interior, and they will not achieve desirable robust growth when they finally emerge.

① ② ③

PLANTING

① *Butomus umbellatus*
② *Lysimachia nummularia* 'Aurea'
③ *Veronica beccabunga*

Mosaic Sink Garden

❧

A water garden in a sink is ideal for the smaller yard or patio.
It looks great placed beside a rock garden planted with tiny alpines,
as the most suitable plants for it are also miniature.

◁ ONE

Cut the tiles into small squares of varying sizes, and sort them into color batches.

▽ TWO

Before you stick the tile pieces to the sink, lay out the mosaic design on a piece of cardboard.

△ THREE

Positioning the tile pieces is a slow process, so apply a generous amount of tile adhesive over only a small area at a time.

△ FOUR

Build up the pattern steadily, attaching the tiles with a slight twisting movement in order to bed them down thoroughly.

YOU WILL NEED

This project utilizes an old sink, but it can be adapted to similar troughs and containers. Before starting work on decoration, block up the plug hole. The hole is not likely to be of a conventional size in an old sink, but if you are lucky you may find a suitable plug. If you do, raise the sink slightly from the ground, perhaps on four bricks, and, when it requires emptying, you can remove the plug and simply let the water drain out. Where a suitable plug cannot be found, block up the hole with a mixture of sand and cement, and paint over it with a sealant.

The materials below are those needed for the feature illustrated here.

- Old sink
- Odd tiles and tile off-cuts freely available from DIY stores
- Good-quality tile adhesive and grout
- Tile cutter
- Aquatic potting mix
- Pea gravel

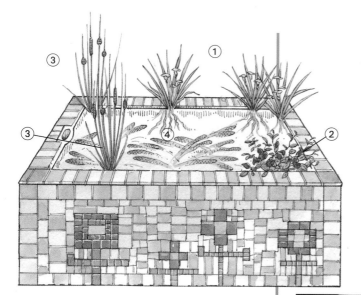

FIVE ▷
When the design
on one side is
complete, wipe
away the grout
with a cloth.
Allow the mosaic
to dry before
continuing with
another side.

THE PLANTS USED

It is easy to overplant a sink, so use a minimal number of plants of the restrained varieties. Even so, they will require regular cutting back during the summer months to keep them compact. There are many plants that can be grown in a sink, but these are the ones used in this feature.

1. *Sisyrinchium californicum var. brachypus*
2. *Mimulus x hybridus* 'Calypso'
3. *Typha minima*
4. *Lagarosiphon major*

◁ **SIX**
When the sides are completed, cap the edge with slightly larger tile pieces. Make sure they are flush with the outside edge.

SEVEN ▷
Finish with a coating of grout, which you must wipe off quickly and smoothly with a damp cloth.

▽ Eight

Allow the sink to dry thoroughly before moving it into position or planting it.

△ Ten

Run water gently into the sink over a piece of plastic in order not to disturb the gravel.

▽ Nine

It is preferable to grow all the plants in containers, or they will become invasive and fill the sink. Spread gravel on the bottom to disguise the white finish and mound it in the corners to form planting positions. Put the plants into position, adjusting the water depth by redistributing the gravel beneath the planting baskets.

△ Eleven

Position a group of submerged plants in the water. The initial cloudiness of the water is caused largely by the gravel, but it will soon settle out and the water will become clear.

Magic in Movement

Bring your patio or garden to life with the sound and color of moving water. Whether it is a gently trickling spray or a bubbling gushing spout, few other elements can change the mood in a garden or patio as radically as moving water sparkling in bright sunshine. Small submersible pumps make it easy to install these features.

Linked with Water

*This barrel garden comprises two half-barrel tubs of different sizes,
positioned so that they create a rustic, flowing water feature.
The turbulent water still allows for a number of planting options.*

The water in this feature is circulated from the lower barrel into an old-fashioned pump from which it cascades down into the two barrels. The ornamental pump is partially encased in the barrels, giving a pleasing unity to the feature. A strong pump is required when creating a feature like this, as there is a considerable lift and substantial water flow.

A container water garden of this kind should be positioned in an open, sunny position. There are some advantages to situating the decorative pump with its back to a wall or in a corner, although it might look a little stark. Alternatively, a position with a shrubby background, or a corner where two hedges meet in a more heavily planted area of your garden would be suitable because of the pump's rustic, Old World appearance.

You can grow a number of plants in the barrels, despite the turbulent water, provided that you select varieties suited to the conditions. The vigorous-growing reedmace, *Typha latifolia*, fits in well here, although it can rarely be grown in other types of container water garden. The area at the back of the lower barrel, where the upper one overlaps it, is an ideal spot. It is sufficiently sheltered for the typha, and its planting basket, filled with aquatic potting mix, can be successfully secured to the barrel so that it does not topple over into the water. In addition, the height of the typha will help to link the barrels visually.

Unlike some other small planted water features, here you can establish creeping plants in the same container as tall marginals such as the typha. *Lysimachia nummularia* 'Aurea', for example, will thrive much better when planted in the bottom of the barrel and tumbling over the edge, rather than being established on its own, when it would need an individual planting basket that would take up limited water space. Combine this planting with other vigorous marginal plants, such as the water plantain, *Alisma plantago-aquatica*. This attractive feature also includes the variegated sweet flag, *Acorus calamus* 'Variegatus', the marsh marigold, *Caltha palustris*, and cheerful tumbling *Veronica beccabunga* to extend the season of interest.

PLANTING

1. *Acorus calamus* 'Variegatus'
2. *Alisma plantago-aquatica*
3. *Caltha palustris*
4. *Lysimachia nummularia* 'Aurea'
5. *Typha latifolia*
6. *Veronica beccabunga*

Pot up a Fountain

❧

Plants are not always necessary in a container water feature. Water trickling gently over stones is evocative of a mountain stream, an effect that can easily be achieved in a small decorative container.

YOU WILL NEED

- Small decorative container
- Plastic bowl or pot with holes
- Submersible pump
- Drilled focal stone
- Pebbles

Many aquatic plants dislike moving water and cannot be used in water gardens with a fountain jet, so in this feature the water itself is the focal point. The container need not be enormous, but it should be able to accommodate a submersible pump in a small chamber with rocks or stones covering the top. An inverted plastic bowl or pot that almost fills the container and comes to within 2–4 inches (5–10cm) of the top is ideal. This should have holes in it to permit the water free passage. Essentially, the decorative pot or bowl is full of water, with the stones or pebbles disguising the chamber from view. The maximum volume of water is essential.

The focal stone in the container should have a hole drilled through it into which you push the pump outlet. Sandstone or limestone are the easiest to drill, although it is possible to buy already drilled stones at specialist aquatics centers. Make sure that the stone is not freshly quarried, but has a hardened, weathered finish, or else it will erode and gritty material will settle in the container and may block the pump.

It is important to check a pebble fountain constantly for water loss. The endless exposure of the water to air and warmth causes a surprising amount of evaporation, and 4–6 inches (10–15cm) of water can be lost in a couple of days. Ideally, the water level should be just above the top of the chamber. The only problem that this can cause is a deposit of algae, rather like a tidemark, along the edge of the stones. To prevent this occurring, and to ensure that the water remains clear and the pebbles fresh and shiny, regularly introduce an organic algicide to the water. This will ensure that the water remains crystal clear and will sparkle in the sunshine.

Going Shishi-odoshi

A shishi-odoshi is a traditional Japanese water feature made from bamboo and operated by moving water. The loud cracking sound that the hollow tube gives was originally intended to scare away deer.

YOU WILL NEED

- Bamboo deer scarer (*shishi-odoshi*)
- Submerged pump
- Large tub or garbage pail to house the pump
- Large pebbles or stones
- Fine wire-mesh reinforcing

PLANTING

1. *Hosta* 'Thomas Hogg'
2. *Iris laevigata* 'Colchesteri'
3. *Onoclea sensibilis*
4. *Primula beesiana*
5. *Primula bulleyana*

There are several configurations for this water feature, but the most usual consists of two upright bamboo supports holding a more slender rocking bamboo tube. Water from a chamber below is pumped up through one of the hollow upright canes, and by means of a small bamboo spout near the top pours into the waiting rocking tube. The weight overbalances the tube forward and the water pours out. In doing this, it knocks against either a strategically positioned short length of bamboo toward the top of the supports, or more usually a stone placed strategically at the bottom.

A chamber sunk into the ground is necessary to operate a *shishi-odoshi*. It should contain a submersible pump that has sufficient power to raise the water without straining. Provided that the pump is completely covered by water, you can use a wide, shallow container. One advantage of this is that it reduces the required lift of the pump; the other that you can accomodate plants that enjoy really wet conditions.

Once the container and pump are installed, position the *shishi-odoshi* close to the side of the sunken container, with the spout pointing toward the middle of it. It is easier to ensure that the upright supports are secure if they are in the ground than if they are fastened to the container. Cover the container with a material such as fine wire-mesh reinforcing, which can support the weight of pebbles or cobbles and is porous at the same time. By enlarging parts of the mesh, provision can be made for plants to grow through it.

There is a wide choice of plants for such a feature, but for the most satisfactory appearance you should choose Japanese plants and those that look Oriental. Use bog garden plants that can stand in water with their crowns just above the surface, or arrange some of the planting in the wet areas near the edge of the feature. *Iris laevigata* 'Colchesteri' can stand very happily in water, but hostas, such as 'Thomas Hogg', *Primula beesiana* and *P. bulleyana*, and the bog garden fern, *Onoclea sensibilis*, are happier in the slightly drier conditions around the edge.

Down by the Old Millstone

A millstone with water bubbling through the center is a pleasing way to enjoy the sound and appearance of water with the benefit of easy maintenance, and, if children are around, perfect safety.

YOU WILL NEED

- Millstone made from fiberglass or reconstituted stone
- Large container or garbage pail
- Submersible pump
- Wire-mesh reinforcing or reinforcing rods
- Pebbles or cobbles
- Planting containers
- Aquatic potting mix

PLANTING

1. *Butomus umbellatus*
2. *Lysimachia nummularia* 'Aurea'
3. *Veronica beccabunga*

Millstone fountains have become a part of many modern gardens. Genuine millstones are few and far between, but in recent years both reconstituted-stone manufacturers and fiberglass molders have set about creating very convincing substitutes. And fiberglass millstones are easily maneuverable, lightweight features.

When preparing to install a millstone water feature choose a shallow container that is at least 6 inches (15cm) larger all round than the millstone. This way you can arrange pebbles or cobbles decoratively around the edge where the overflowing water seeps through, and one or two places where plants can be introduced are provided.

Sink the container into the ground and install a submersible pump. Attach a piece of string to the outlet tube so that in due course it can be pulled through the center of the millstone. You must provide a secure base for the millstone to rest on; this can be made from either wire-mesh reinforcing or metal reinforcing rods. A large-gauge mesh is required for the main support, and you will also need finer mesh material to lay over the top to prevent pebbles from dropping through the gaps. Once the support system is in place, position the millstone carefully and draw the string fastened to the outlet through the center of the stone so that a simple jet can be attached to it. Then place pebbles or cobbles around the millstone to disguise the pump chamber completely.

As the millstone is such a strong feature on its own, any associated planting must be carefully arranged. Use more discrete plants such as *Veronica beccabunga* and *Lysimachia nummularia* 'Aurea' around the edge to soften the appearance of the pebbles, and slender plants such as *Butomus umbellatus* to provide height. You can establish these plants in low, flat containers and place them on top of the reinforced support, surrounding and covering them with pebbles. Alternatively, you can position them within the chamber and raise their containers on bricks. However, this reduces the water volume and means that the plants have to emerge between the reinforcing, which is not always satisfactory. It is much easier to control them if they are planted among the pebbles.

Pocketing the Best

A traditional strawberry pot can be turned into an attractive water feature if lined with a piece of pool liner or a waterproof pot insert. Plant the outside pockets with luscious trailing plants.

YOU WILL NEED

- Strawberry pot
- Submersible pump
- Pool liner or plastic insert
- Adhesive
- General-purpose potting mix

Ideally you should use a plastic pot insert for this feature as it has the necessary rigidity. If you cannot find a suitable sized insert, a piece of pool liner will do the job. Make sure that it is kept safely in place by sticking the liner to the inside of the strawberry pot with adhesive, and neatly finish off the edge.

Water is circulated by a miniature submersible pump that weighs about 1lb (500g) and nestles neatly in the bottom of the pot. Carefully slip down the cable between the insert and the inner wall of the pot and thread it through one of the lower planting holes that will be turned away from the main line of view.

The pockets in the pot should be filled with general-purpose potting mix. Unlike a conventionally planted strawberry pot, there is no opportunity to work both inside and outside the pot and you will have to insert the potting mix and each plant from the outside. As there is relatively little potting mix available for each plant, you have to select suitable plant types and water them regularly. The constant dampness of the clay pot does assist with humidity.

The trailing *Lobelia erinus* is one of the most suitable plants for this kind of feature. It tolerates having only a little soil for its roots and produces good-quality foliage and masses of blue flowers throughout most of the summer. To ensure that it continues to flower well once the small amount of potting mix has become exhausted, apply a foliar feed regularly. Any liquid feed applied to the sparse amount of soil in the pockets is likely to be wasted, since most of it will simply run down the outside of the pot, but fertilizer tablets are a good alternative.

You can also try using trailing plants that are grown for their attractive tumbling foliage rather than their flowers, especially the golden-leafed *Lysimachia nummularia* 'Aurea' and its green-leafed, yellow-flowered parent *L. nummularia*.

PLANTING

1 *Lobelia erinus* 'Blue Trailing'

Be Classical!

Fountain masks offer great opportunities for introducing moving water into a limited space, especially where the area is surrounded by a wall, fence, or trellis.

You Will Need

- Lion's head wall mask
- Submersible pump
- Plastic pail
- Paving slabs
- Ball valve (optional)

Planting

① *Mimulus luteus*
② *Pontederia cordata*
③ *Potamogeton crispus*
   (submerged)

Although the fountain mask is simple to fix, you must ensure that it functions properly. You could introduce a submersible pump into the small pool into which the mask spouts, but it is difficult to disguise the pump and the outflow up to the mask. When installing this kind of feature, it is better to construct a proper lower chamber to accommodate the pump safely. A standard plastic pail is an ideal receptacle.

Sink the pail into the ground and place the pool for the fountain on paving slabs placed over the top of the pail. Arrange these carefully so that you are able to gain access to the pump when necessary. Often the pool will be provided with an overflow, rather like that on a kitchen sink, which links into the sump below; if it does not have a built-in overflow, you will need to construct one. The pump circulates the water up into the mask, from where it drops down into the pool and then overflows back into the sump. The water level in the sump will require regular topping up, which is simply a matter of running a hose into it periodically. It is also quite easy to contrive a ball valve arrangement in the sump itself, which will ensure that it is topped up automatically.

Arranging the outlet so that it is not seen can take some ingenuity, but on a fence or trellis it is fairly easy since the mask has to be fastened to an upright to secure it and the outlet can be hidden behind the same upright. Where the mask is fastened to a wall it is a little more difficult. With a plasterboard wall a hole must be drilled through it so that the outlet pipe can be passed up out of sight behind it; solid walls can usually accommodate the pipe in the central cavity.

Aquatics with floating leaves and true floating plants dislike the conditions in a fountain pool with constantly running water. It is much better to use marginal plants, such as the yellow musk, *Mimulus luteus*, and stately pickerel, *Pontederia cordata*, together with occasional submerged aquatics such as *Potamogeton crispus*, which are tolerant of disturbed water.

Pouring Water

The tilted urn appears as if it has been left lying on its side and the water it contains is spilling out. It is seated on pebbles in a container, with a pump situated beneath.

YOU WILL NEED

- Ceramic or terra-cotta urn
- Plastic or polypropylene container
- Submersible pump
- Wire-mesh reinforcing
- Weed-suppressing fabric
- Pebbles or cobbles

PLANTING

① *Caltha palustris* 'Flore Pleno'
② *Iris laevigata* 'Variegata'
③ *Lobelia* x *speciosa* 'Queen Victoria'
④ *Mimulus* x *hybridus* 'Malibu'

For this feature, the pump connection is discreetly arranged at the lower end of the urn and water spills from the rim, so the whole urn has to be seated within a base container to avoid loss of water.

Any container can be used as a base, either raised or sunken. The lower container is not only the chamber from which water is circulated with a submerged pump but it also provides sufficient room to establish complementary marginal or bog plants.

If the container is sunk into the ground, it need only be of strong plastic or polypropylene, and will, therefore, be light and easy to install. Position the pump on the bottom of the container and disguise the cable with paving, pebbles, or plants where it emerges. Install the plants in their pots on the floor of the container and then place strong wire-mesh reinforcing over the top so that it covers the entire surface of the container, with the plants just poking through. Put a layer of weed-suppressing fabric over the top, with holes cut in it where the plants emerge and some small slits made in other areas to allow the water to filter through to the container beneath. Then cover the area with pebbles. The pebbles can be restricted to the surface of the container, defining it clearly, or can be spread beyond its edge so that it looks as if the tilted urn is lying on the ground.

Although an attractive feature on its own, it looks much better when dressed with plants of varying growth habits. Use the double-flowered marsh marigold, *Caltha palustris* 'Flore Pleno', for an early spring show. Follow this with the blue-flowered *Iris laevigata* with its handsome swordlike leaves, which form a striking contrast to the red-purple foliage of *Lobelia* x *speciosa* 'Queen Victoria'. The easygoing, summer-long flowering *Mimulus* x *hybridus* 'Malibu' is an attractive addition. Alternative plants for this feature include *Caltha palustris* 'Alba' and *Typha minima* with its grassy foliage and small brown poker heads.

Trickling Trio

If properly arranged, this is one of the most visually appealing water features. It has a pebbled area with strategically placed bubbling pots and occasional planting to soften the harshness of the stones.

The pumps for this project need to be installed in the pots without the cable being visible. In order to achieve this, you need either to drill holes in the pots through which to thread the cable, or else to use the drainage holes in the base of the pots and seal in the cable with epoxy glue. Alternatively, a stronger single pump can be installed in a sunken chamber and three outlets provided through the drainage holes.

The latter method means that you have to sink a large container or tank into the ground, ideally something like a water butt or storage tank. Set the pump in the tank just beneath the maximum water level so that it is completely submerged. Place a sheet of heavy-gauge, fine wire-mesh reinforcing over the tank and position the outlet pipes so that they emerge close to the drainage holes in the pots. Then thread the pipes through the drainage holes and secure and waterproof them with an epoxy glue. Cover the mesh with pebbles, leaving places for aquatic planting baskets to be inserted into the mesh. Arrange the pebbles carefully around the baskets so that they are not visible.

There are many plants to choose from, but it is pleasant to have a few creeping specimens, such as *Lysimachia nummularia* 'Aurea', to soften the harshness of the pebbles, and some upright spears of leafy growth to provide contrast. The variegated *Acorus calamus* and dwarf *A. gramineus* are ideal, and so is the common blue-flowered Japanese iris, *Iris laevigata*. Alternatively, *Sagittaria sagittifolia* and *Pontederia cordata* are equally suitable to the conditions provided, and so is *Iris laevigata* 'Colchesteri' with its bold, dark-purple and white flowers.

PLANTING

1. *Acorus calamus* 'Variegatus'
2. *Acorus gramineus* 'Variegatus'
3. *Iris laevigata*
4. *Lysimachia nummularia* 'Aurea'

Cool but Colorful

❧

This miniature water garden allows you to grow a range of plants in a limited space, combined with moving water. It is an ideal feature for an open, sunny position on a patio or in a courtyard garden.

◁ **ONE**

Cut the timber to size, then paint it with a wood preservative and allow it to dry before tacking the base to the sides with brads.

TWO ▷

Secure the top corners with joint blocks. Make sure that they will not interfere with the top molding.

THREE ▷

Attach the split fence posts to the base with screws from the inside. Then turn the container over and screw the base to the sides. The split fence posts raise the container off the ground.

YOU WILL NEED

This project can be modified to suit your requirements. You can make it in a different size or even in an "L" shape if you prefer.

- Two 36in (90cm) and two 18in (45cm) lengths of 10 x 1in (25 x 2.5cm) timber
- 36 x 20in (90 x 50cm) piece of ½in (12.5mm) exterior plywood
- Two 40in (1m) and two 24in (60cm) lengths of decorative molding
- Two 20in (50cm) lengths of split fence post
- Colored water-soluble wood preservative
- Brads
- 4 corner joint blocks
- Pool liner
- Staple gun
- Sharp knife
- Plastic container (for pump)
- Screws to fit the joint blocks
- Hammer, screwdriver, drill
- Submersible pump
- Aquatic potting mix
- Pea gravel

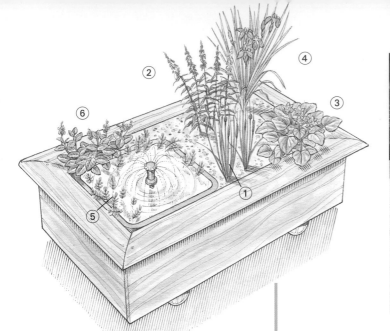

THE PLANTS USED

There are many different plants that can be used for this project, but you must curb your enthusiasm and be careful not to overplant. Planting at the correct spacing may look sparse for a month or more, but the plants will quickly mature. An overplanted feature of this kind would not be a success.

1. *Typha minima*
2. *Lobelia* x *speciosa* 'Queen Victoria'
3. *Caltha palustris* 'Flore Pleno'
4. *Iris laevigata*
5. *Myriophyllum aquaticum*
6. *Veronica beccabunga*

Alternative plants suitable for this feature:
Acorus calamus 'Variegatus'
Primula sikkimensis

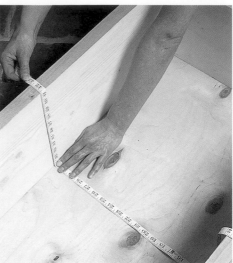

◁ FOUR

Measure the box and prepare the liner to fit. Make it slightly larger than required.

◁ FIVE

Fit the liner carefully into the box and attach it with staples. Trim off any surplus material with a sharp knife.

SIX ▷

Cut the end of the moldings at a 45-degree angle to ensure a snug fit. Using a fine bit, drill holes for the screws through the moldings. Then hold the moldings in position and screw them securely to the box walls.

SEVEN ▷

In one end, place a waterproof plastic container large enough to accommodate the pump, about 10 inches (25cm) deep. Fill in around the plastic container with aquatic planting mix. Alternatively, and more economically, you can fill the lower 6 inches (15cm) of the feature with pea gravel and put planting mix on top.

◁ EIGHT

Remove the plants from their containers and plant them directly into the potting mix.

△ NINE

When all the plants have been put in position, top-dress the surface of the planting mix with a generous layer of pea gravel.

◁ TEN

Fill the plastic container with water and place the submersible pump in it, with the cable discreetly tucked beneath the molding and ideally hidden by some foliage.

Going with the Flow

❧

This feature provides a perfect opportunity to bring moving water to the patio in a natural way. The container is made from timber lined with a pool liner, but you can use any waterproof container of suitable size.

YOU WILL NEED

- Timber box
- Pool liner
- Rocks or preformed cascade unit
- Submersible pump
- Plastic aquatic planting container or large pot with holes
- Stones
- Plastic windbreak netting
- Aquatic potting mix

Simplicity is the keynote here, as the focus should be on the stone forming the cascade in the center of this feature. This focal point can be constructed either from pieces of stone, as shown here, or from a preformed cascade unit. Stone works much better in this design and gives the gardener greater freedom to work with the water flow. Be careful what type of stone you choose, as soft materials such as sandstone and freshly quarried limestone can make the water cloudy.

Once the timber box has been put in position, and made watertight with pool liner, the construction of the stone centerpiece can begin. Make sure that there is an electricity supply nearby and that the container is level and in the open. Place the submersible pump in position and invert a plastic aquatic planting container or a large pot with holes over the pump to protect it. Also check that the water is deep enough to cover the pump completely, as it must be submerged at all times. Then erect the stone feature around and over the pump.

The way in which the stones and plantings are arranged is a matter of personal taste, but ideally the water should emerge from the cascade at one end of the feature and be directed so that it produces the effect of a small stream. Of course, the stream will not go anywhere—it will just appear to be moving, due to the turbulence created at one end. Make the edge of the stream from smaller pieces of stone. Behind the stones, and disguised by them, place a barrier of fine plastic windbreak netting and behind that pack in aquatic potting mix in which to grow your plants. The netting will prevent the compost from spilling into the stream.

You can set the plants directly into the potting mix on either side of the stream. Here, *Iris versicolor* 'Kermesina' and *I. laevigata* 'Rose Queen' have been used to give height, while the marsh marigold, *Caltha palustris*, provides early color. The careful arrangement of *Calla palustris* softens the rocky edges of the stream.

PLANTING

① *Iris laevigata* 'Rose Queen'
② *Iris versicolor* 'Kermesina'
③ *Caltha palustris*
④ *Calla palustris*

Indoor and Conservatory

Bringing water inside is a relatively recent,
but very welcome invention. Not only can you
enjoy the pleasures of water all year round,
the range of plants to associate with it is also
much larger than outdoors. Whether in the
living room or conservatory, the presence of
water is a delight, creating humidity and
flowers for your pleasure.

Spouting Forth

A frog sitting on a lily pad and spouting water entertains everyone, whatever their age. Part of the charm of this feature is the somewhat startled appearance that vigorously spouting water gives to the frog.

YOU WILL NEED

- Spouting frog
- Terra-cotta or ceramic container
- Submersible pump
- Aquatic potting mix
- Pebbles (optional)
- Pot with holes around the side (optional)

Gardening should be fun. Although many traditional gardeners believe that only plants and natural materials should be used in the garden, if we look back through history we see that the odd, bizarre, and amusing frequently appear, especially in the form of statuary.

Any container can be utilized for a fountain such as this, but as the frog is to be the center of attention, the container should preferably be made from subdued, mellow-colored terra-cotta or ceramic. A strongly colored or busily patterned container will detract from the frog.

Although the frog ornament can be situated anywhere in the container it is better to put it at the side so that full justice can be done to the spouting water. If you place the frog in the center of the container, you will have to reduce the pressure on the pump jet so that the water does not splash over the edge. The water can spout into a bowl that contains water, with space for a couple of plants, or the bowl can be filled with pebbles. If you decide on the latter, you must install an inverted pot with holes around the side to create a sump for the pump, and seat the frog and lily pad on top of this arrangement. However, most gardeners will prefer the lily pad to appear as if it is floating on open water.

Used indoors, such a feature will provide invaluable humidity in a dry atmosphere and it will allow you to plant interesting subtropical marginal plants that might be too tender to plant outdoors, such as the lovely yellow-flowered small arum, *Zantedeschia elliottiana*. This is a superb plant, and it provides a telling contrast to the grassy, somewhat filigree foliage of *Cyperus isocladus*.

PLANTING

① *Cyperus isocladus*
② *Zantedeschia elliottiana*

Percolating Through

The appeal of this small water feature lies in the feeling of movement, the color of the wet stone, and the attractive ceramic container. Putting it together demands a little care, but it's worth the effort.

For this feature, the pump is situated in the center of the container and is covered by an inverted pot with holes in the side or an inverted plastic planting basket, to allow water to percolate through. This forms a chamber around the pump so that soil and stones cannot interfere with its working.

The plants are placed into squares of burlap or discarded pantyhose containing aquatic potting mix. Pantyhose are ideal, as they can be cut to size, filled with potting mix, and then tied up, and the plants can be inserted through small holes cut in the fabric. The fine weave of the pantyhose prevents the potting mix from seeping out and polluting the water, and it is also very flexible and molds easily to the spaces around the pump chamber. It is important in such a restricted space that you choose plants whose root systems will adapt to such constraints.

It is a good idea to wedge the chamber with two or three sizable stones before inserting the plants. Once you have decided on the position of the plants, put them in and place fairly large pebbles around and over the top of the planting bags to disguise them completely. The main focal stone, already drilled, is then positioned on the top and the outlet of the pump fed into it. Use a main stone of sandstone or limestone, but make sure that it is well weathered and has a hard outer coat so that the water does not gradually erode it and produce a gritty deposit that may get into the pump. Freshly quarried stone often looks bright and clean, but may wear away quickly.

Use a combination of plants with an upright habit for this feature, but include at least one scrambling plant such as the parrot feather, *Myriophyllum aquaticum*, to hide the edge. The best plants for introducing a little height and character are the double-flowered arrowhead, *Sagittaria sagittifolia* 'Flore Pleno', the corkscrew rush, *Juncus effusus* 'Spiralis', and the dwarf Japanese *Typha minima*. All of these plants are very attractive when grown together and are reliable when their roots are restricted as they are here.

PLANTING

1. *Juncus effusus* 'Spiralis'
2. *Myriophyllum aquaticum*
3. *Typha minima*
4. *Sagittaria sagittifolia* 'Flore Pleno'

Music and Movement

❧

This is an attractive, ready-made indoor water feature where the water flows gently around and across the metal leaves. For the best effect place it in a well-lit position or focus a spotlight on it.

YOU WILL NEED
- Ready-made water feature with metal leaves
- Crushed charcoal (filter carbon)
- Aquatic potting mix
- Discarded pantyhose
- Artificial plants (optional)

This feature contains a discreet pump that you merely have to plug in and switch on to start the function. Although it is beautifully sculpted, it does benefit from softening with select plants set in the bowl.

A small indoor feature like this will lose a considerable amount of moisture through evaporation and so you need to top it up continually with fresh water. In order to keep the water sweet and prevent it from becoming stale, add a tablespoonful of fine charcoal, such as that used in aquarium filters, which is known as filter carbon. In such a small volume of water, particularly where it is constantly moving, it is difficult to raise water quality by introducing submerged plants. While they would thrive, they would almost certainly become an unseemly tangle. In this feature, the container has been filled with attractive pebbles, to complement the plants, give it additional stability, and help to overcome potential problems with water clarity.

There are only a few tender plants that occupy little space and and can be used to dress the bowl, but varieties of *Acorus gramineus* and the dwarf-growing *Cyperus isocladus* are perfect for the job. However, they need careful preparation and placement. Fortunately, these plants can exist with a very modest amount of growing medium, and by wrapping the roots of each plant in a generous handful of aquatic potting mix in a piece of old pantyhose and securing it firmly, you can fit the plants into the bowl without causing any spillage or polluting the water.

In the case of a small feature such as this one, there is some advantage in considering artificial plants, particularly as the better-quality ones are not affected by the water or temperature, and can be used in awkward places. Here, artificial ivy has been twined around the stems of the metal leaves to give the feature an attractive, more natural appearance.

PLANTING
① *Acorus gramineus* 'Ogon'
② *Cyperus isocladus*

Terrific for the Sideboard

❧

This is more a humidifier than a water feature, but, if a deep enough bowl is selected, there is no reason why it cannot be turned into a miniature water garden.

YOU WILL NEED

- Ceramic or
  terra-cotta bowl
- Submersible pump
- Small pot with holes
- Pebbles
- Focal drilled stone
- Crushed charcoal (filter
  carbon)
- Discarded pantyhose
- Aquatic potting mix

This type of water feature is often referred to as a tabletop fountain, although where there is access all around the table this can cause a problem, as there is an electric cable that must be disguised. It is better used as a sideboard decoration, where the wire can be tucked discreetly out of sight.

The pump is positioned in a small chamber that can easily be created out of an upturned pot. It must have holes through which the water can pass. Although the bowl can contain open water, it is better to pack well-washed pebbles around the chamber to disguise it. On top of this, set the waterfall stone, which has a hole drilled in the upper part through which the pump outlet is installed.

The top layer of pebbles is very important, as it can enhance this feature visually or make it look quite ordinary. The pebbles should be of roughly equal size and of a color that pleasingly echoes the color of the central waterfall stone. Adding a little charcoal to the water will keep it sweet and clear. Use a tablespoonful of crushed charcoal, such as that sold for aquariums as filter carbon. This should overcome the occasional problem of odor, and reduces possible algal discoloration of the pebbles.

Establish the plants in aquatic potting mix wrapped up in pieces of discarded pantyhose. This way, dwarf-growing plants such as the varieties of *Acorus gramineus* and the diminutive *Cyperus isocladus* can become well established, even though they are packed around with pebbles. *Pleioblastus pygmaeus* is an excellent alternative for planting this feature.

During the winter months ensure that the plants receive sufficient light. When kept in a well-lit position, they will remain evergreen and in character. If they do not make it through the winter, you would do best to dispose of them, pull the feature apart, and reassemble it without any plants until the following spring.

PLANTING

① *Acorus gramineus*
  'Variegatus'
② *Cyperus isocladus*

Raising the Sights

The simple planting and the rustic construction of this pool provide the focal point for a colorfully planted area. The water flowing over the rocky cascade brings a touch of the countryside to the garden.

◁ ONE

Place the hexagonal base on the floor and screw the sides on to it, using 12 jointing blocks and ½in (12.5mm) screws.

▽ TWO

Position the cascade waterfall unit on the top hexagon, which has yet to be fixed, and draw around it, leaving about 1½ inches (4cm) for support. Cut out the shape with a jigsaw.

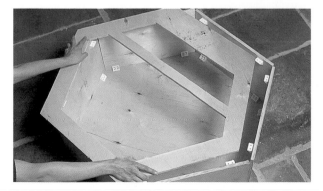

△ THREE

Screw the other 12 jointing blocks in place around the top, and then screw the top hexagon into position, using ½in (12.5mm) screws.

YOU WILL NEED

This project can be adjusted to any size, but it will be quite heavy when completed and so it is better to build larger constructions in situ.

The materials below are those needed for the feature illustrated here.

- Six 18 x 12in (45 x 30cm) pieces of ½in (12.5mm) exterior plywood
- 2 hexagons of ½in (12.5mm) exterior plywood with 18in (45cm) sides
- Thirty 18in (45cm) lengths of 3 x 1in (7.5 x 2.5cm) fencing rails
- Pool liner
- 24 jointing blocks
- ½in (12.5mm) and 1in (2.5cm) screws
- Nails (optional)
- Colored water-soluble wood preservative
- Screwdriver, hammer (optional), staple gun, jigsaw
- Pea gravel
- Aquatic potting mix
- Bricks or inverted planting baskets

THE PLANTS USED

The success of this design depends largely on its rustic appearance and the simplicity of moving water, so few plants are used. For the best effect, position two graceful-looking flowering plants of the same kind at the sides of the cascade unit. Alternatively, you could use sentinel-like plants such as *Iris laevigata* varieties, which would give it a more severe appearance, although for a short period of time there would be a colorful floral display. You could add a floating aquatic plant, but avoid a carpeting kind such as azolla. Submerged aquatics, such as *Myriophyllum aquaticum*, add additional interest.

① *Carex elata* 'Bowles' Golden'

② *Stratiotes aloides*

③ *Myriophyllum aquaticum*

◁ **FOUR**
To add strength, screw the sides directly into the top and base with 1in (2.5cm) screws. Then paint them with a colored wood preservative.

FIVE ▷
Paint the rails with a contrasting colored wood preservative and secure them with 1in (2.5cm) nails or screws.

◁ **SIX**
Cut the pool liner to shape and insert it carefully into the construction. Fasten it to the underside of the top hexagon with a staple gun.

◁ SEVEN

Site the completed container, ready for planting, in an open sunny position.

▽ NINE

Once the plants are in place you can secure the cascade unit by drilling a hole and screwing it into the base. Drill another hole in the back of the cascade unit to take the pump outlet.

EIGHT ▷

Remove the plants carefully from their pots and place them in aquatic planting baskets filled with aquatic potting mix. Cover the surfaces with fine gravel. Position them in the container, bringing them up to the right level by standing them on inverted planting baskets or bricks.

△ TEN

Fill the box with water and position the pump in the container. Connect the pump outlet to the cascade unit through the drilled hole, and the cable to the electrical supply.

Spice it Up!

The herb cluster pot is a traditional container water garden feature. These united terra-cotta pots are perfect for a moving water feature for indoors, or for a temporary summer arrangement outside.

You Will Need

- Terra-cotta herb cluster pot
- Large decorative bowl
- Submersible pump
- Large pot with holes, or fine-mesh wire netting
- Pebbles
- Aquatic potting mix
- Discarded pantyhose
- Artificial plants (optional)

The large bowl in this feature serves as a reservoir for the pump, which is placed on the bottom. The pump can be protected by enclosing it with a large inverted pot with holes, through which the outlet hose passes and water can flow back in.

Alternatively, you can use screwed-up fine-mesh wire netting. It might not look particularly strong, but in sufficient quantity it forms a stable reinforcing on which you can place the surface pebbles and the terra-cotta herb cluster pots. Fix a small plastic insert into the base of the center pot to serve as the pump hose connector, and push the outlet hose from the submersible pump into it.

The plants are grown in aquatic potting mix, wrapped in pieces of old pantyhose that are then securely knotted. This allows the plants to develop their own rootballs without the potting mix discoloring the water. You can then mold the rootballs into the space available and place pebbles around the plants to cover them up.

The plants used in this feature are a combination of fairly tender and suitable hardy kinds. *Cyperus isocladus* is a tropical plant that can stand quite cool temperatures. *Acorus gramineus* 'Ogon' is hardy but suffers if winters are severe, while the scrambling *Lysimachia nummularia* 'Aurea' is completely hardy. With such a plant combination you need to be careful to maintain the correct temperature, as too much warmth, especially in the absence of good light, leads to a distortion of growth. If winter conditions indoors are too dull and the plants appear to suffer, it is preferable to remove them completely and rebuild the feature so that it is plantless until the spring.

Although no self-respecting gardener would normally wish to utilize artificial plant material, in instances where a water feature looks stark without green foliage there are good reasons for experimenting with some of the high-quality artificial specimens that are now available. In some conditions, where live plants suffer, it may be the best solution.

Planting

1. *Acorus gramineus* 'Ogon'
2. *Cyperus isocladus*
3. *Lysimachia nummularia* 'Aurea'

Corner Piece

❧

This movable water feature is ideal for bringing water into a greenhouse. It can be used with a fountain jet, but it is equally attractive as a planted feature without moving water.

ONE ▷

Screw and glue the front and sides to the base, using 12 jointing blocks and ½in (12.5mm) screws.

△ **TWO**

With a jigsaw, cut the shape of the pond out of the upper triangle. Leave a 6in (15cm) wide shelf along two sides.

◁ **THREE**

Position the upper triangle on top of the other, and apply glue around the top rim.

YOU WILL NEED

You can adapt this project to suit almost any situation. It is a simple matter to make it deeper or longer. In this case, it is small enough to be easily portable.

- 48 x 48in (1.5 x 1.5m) square of ½in (12.5mm) exterior plywood, cut diagonally to create two triangles
- Two 48 x 12in (1.5m x 30cm), and one 69 x 12in (1.75m x 30cm) lengths of ½in (12.5mm) exterior plywood
- 69in (1.75m) length of decorative molding
- Two 36in (90cm) lengths of trellising
- 12 jointing blocks
- 2in (5cm) and ½in (12.5mm) screws
- Glue
- Brads
- Colored water-soluble wood preservative
- Hammer, screwdriver, drill, jigsaw, staple gun
- Pool liner
- Aquatic potting mix
- Pea gravel
- Bricks or aquatic planting baskets

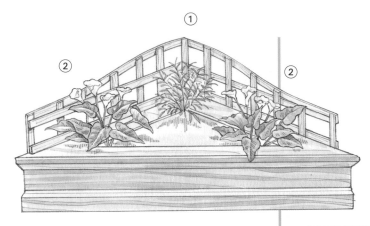

FOUR ▷
Pin the top securely into position, using a hammer and brads.

THE PLANTS USED

Only a limited number of aquatic plants can be used in a pool of this kind, as most tropical plants grow too big and boisterous to be suitable. Apart from aquatic plants, you can use a wide range of decorative indoor plants on the shelves to create an ever-changing display. Most plants will benefit from the localized humidity created by the pool. If you use plants that tolerate low light levels, this feature could also be kept indoors.

① *Pleioblastus pygmaeus*
② *Zantedeschia aethiopica*

Alternative plants suitable for this feature:
Cyperus isocladus
Zantedeschia elliottiana

◁ **FIVE**
Paint the whole container with wood preservative and allow to dry. Then attach the molding to the front edges of the pool with screws from the inside.

SIX ▷
Pre-drill holes in the trellis to prevent the wood from splitting, and screw the two lengths to the back of the pool to form a corner.

SEVEN ▷

Cut the pool liner slightly larger than is required, and trim off the surplus once installed. Arrange the liner carefully by hand, and staple it underneath the inside edge of the pool using the staple gun.

△ EIGHT

The pool is now ready for planting. Use bricks or inverted planting baskets as supports in the corners where you are planning to place the plants.

TEN ▷

Add water to the pool, taking care not to disturb the plants.

▽ NINE

Plant the aquatic plants in baskets containing aquatic potting mix, and cover the top with pea gravel. Carefully place the baskets on their supports in the pool.

Directory of Plants

This directory is not exhaustive, but it gives a selection of the range of subjects that can be used for container water gardening. Your choices will be governed by the shape of your container, and, in the case of an outdoor feature, by climatic considerations. The plants described here are largely trouble-free and will not swamp the confined growing conditions of small containers.

How to Use the Directory

The plants in the Directory are listed alphabetically by their Latin names. All the information you need about the plant is contained under the headings described here. The variety of aquatic plants that are suitable for container water gardens are numerous. Those selected here are the best for the widest range of climates and conditions.

When purchasing aquatic plants, be sure that they are nursery grown. Some cheaper plants have often been removed from the wild and are not only illegally traded, but are more difficult to establish. They can also introduce undesirable pests and diseases to your water feature.

① **Botanical names** are international and the forms given are the ones usually used in nurseries and garden centers.

② **Common name** is the name used by most people to refer to the plant.

③ **Minimum winter temperature** is the lowest temperature a plant can survive at. It is important to remember that these are only guides. A plant's ability to survive certain temperatures is also affected by factors like protection from the wind.

④ **Zone** Each plant has a number or range of numbers that corresponds with the hardiness zone maps on pages 114–15.

⑤ **Characteristics** describes the general growth habit and both foliage and flowers of the plant, together with the expected height in a single season. Floating aquatic plants and deep-water aquatics like waterlilies are denoted as a spread across the surface of the water.

⑥ **Cultivation** gives details of specific requirements, along with notes on propagation.

The moisture-loving Primula beesiana.

① *PRIMULA DENTICULATA* ②
(Drumstick primula)

MINIMUM TEMPERATURE –4°F (–20°C) ③
④ ZONE **6**

CHARACTERISTICS ⑤
A well-known primula that is often grown in the mixed border. Large globular heads of lilac, pink, purple, or white flowers are borne on stout stems. The leaves are green, large, and coarse, with a distinctive aroma and often smothered beneath with a white meal that also extends up the flower stems. Dies back completely during the winter. Height 12–24 inches (30–60cm).

CULTIVATION ⑥
Grow in full sun or partial shade in a damp, richly organic soil. After flowering, remove the old flower heads to prevent self-seeding. Every three or four years lift, divide, and replant as soon as flowering is over. Propagation is from seed sown in a cold frame as soon as it ripens. Seed kept for spring sowing will usually require freezing for about three weeks in order to break its dormancy.

Symbols at the top of each plant entry give the following information at a quick glance:

Deep-water aquatics are those plants that grow on the floor of the pool or water feature and produce leaves that float on the surface of the water, such as waterlilies. Although described as deep-water aquatics, they do tolerate the shallows of a container water feature. The difference is that they do not produce aerial foliage.

Marginal plants are those that usually grow in the water at the edge of a pool. They are tolerant of standing water or very wet conditions all year-round. They are the most important group of plants for container water features.

Bog plants differ from marginal plants in that they will not tolerate standing water, especially during the winter. They require very damp soil.

Floating plants are those aquatics that float around freely on the surface of the water. They derive their nourishment from the water and often sink and take the form of a turion or winter bud in the autumn.

 Submerged plants grow completely beneath the water, although they may produce flowers on the surface. It is these plants that help to keep the water clear and sweet.

Flowering period (if applicable)

Spring   Summer   Autumn   Cross-seasonal

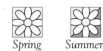 **Weediness** These plants may be classified as weeds in some countries. Weediness is not necessarily a detriment. It indicates that a particular plant, if left to its own devices, may swamp its less vigorous neighbours. There is also the danger that, if allowed to escape into the wild, it will become a nuisance.

Winter hardiness This denotes the degree of tolerance of cold that a plant will take before it is damaged. Occasionally, if there are variations of cold and relative warmth during the winter months, a plant may succumb at a higher temperature. It may have been induced to start growing before being hit by cold weather again.

Full sun Requires full sun

Light shade Tolerates light shade

The striking orchid primula,
Primula vialii.

ACORUS CALAMUS 'VARIEGATUS'
(Variegated sweet flag)

MINIMUM TEMPERATURE **5°F (–15°C)**
ZONE **7**

CHARACTERISTICS
Very hardy marginal aquatic plant with cream, green, and rose-flushed, boldly variegated sword-shaped, irislike leaves. These have a strong tangerine fragrance if bruised. The first shoots in spring take on a bright crimson hue and arise from fat, fleshy rhizomes. The insignificant yellowish-green hornlike flower spikes appear among the foliage during midsummer. Height 36–48 inches (90–120cm).

CULTIVATION
Grow in moist soil or up to 2 inches (5cm) of water in an open, sunny position. Propagation is by division of the fleshy rhizomes during the active growing season. Only plant vigorous young fans of leaves. Discard old woody rhizomes.

ACORUS GRAMINEUS 'MINIMUS'

MINIMUM TEMPERATURE **21°F (–6°C)**
ZONE **9**

CHARACTERISTICS
Semi-evergreen, marginal plant with small, grassy, deep green leaves. Insignificant hornlike flower spikes are occasionally produced among the foliage during summer. In frost-free conditions, the plant is evergreen. If temperatures fall below freezing, it dies back or, in many cases, disappears completely, especially when in standing water. Height up to 3 inches (8cm).

CULTIVATION
Grow in moist soil or up to ¾ inch (2cm) of water in an open, sunny position. Grows best in a frost-free environment in a greenhouse or conservatory with a minimum temperature of around 55°F (13°C). Propagation is by dividing established plants during spring or early autumn.

ACORUS GRAMINEUS 'OGON'

MINIMUM TEMPERATURE **21°F (–6°C)**
ZONE **9**

CHARACTERISTICS
Semi-evergreen, marginal aquatic plant with small, narrow irislike leaves variegated with chartreuse and cream. The tiny hornlike flower spikes are produced sparingly among the foliage during midsummer, but are rarely noticed. In frost-free conditions, the plant is evergreen, responding well to subtropical temperatures. If temperatures fall below freezing, it dies back to its small wiry creeping rhizome and does not reappear until the following spring. Height up to 4 inches (10cm).

CULTIVATION
Grow in moist soil or up to ¾ inch (2cm) of water in an open, sunny position, or preferably in a greenhouse where the minimum temperature is 55°F (13°C). Propagation is by dividing established plants during spring or early autumn.

ACORUS GRAMINEUS 'VARIEGATUS'
(Variegated dwarf sweet flag)

MINIMUM TEMPERATURE **21°F (–6°C)**
ZONE **9**

CHARACTERISTICS
Semi-evergreen, variegated, marginal aquatic plant with small, narrow irislike leaves strikingly variegated with dark green and cream. The small hornlike flowers are insignificant and only noticed by the most observant gardener. In frost-free conditions, the plant remains lush and evergreen. When temperatures fall below freezing, it often dies back to its tiny rhizome and reappears in the following spring. Height up to 4 inches (10cm).

CULTIVATION
Grow in moist soil or with up to ¾ inch (2cm) of water in an open sunny position. Although reasonably hardy, it is best cultivated in subtropical conditions with a temperature of around 55°F (13°C). Propagation is by division of established clumps during spring or early autumn.

ALISMA LANCEOLATUM
(Narrow-leafed water plantain)

MINIMUM TEMPERATURE **–4°F (–20°C)**
ZONE **6**

CHARACTERISTICS
Very hardy marginal plant with dark green, lance-shaped or elliptical leaves arising from neat, nonspreading clumps. The slender branched spires of pink three-petaled flowers are produced during midsummer. The plant dies down completely during the winter. Height 16–24 inches (40–60cm).

CULTIVATION
Grow in moist soil or up to 6 inches (15cm) of water in an open, sunny position. As soon as flowering is over remove the faded flower spikes, as these will set seed that will spread freely and can become a nuisance. Propagation is by dividing established clumps of plants during spring, or from seed sown as soon as it ripens.

ALISMA PLANTAGO-AQUATICA
(Water plantain)

MINIMUM TEMPERATURE **–4°F (–20°C)**
ZONE **6**

CHARACTERISTICS
Very hardy marginal plant producing bright green, oval leaves that are held upright through the water. It grows in neat clumps from among which loose pyramidal spires of white or pinkish papery flowers are produced. Once flowering is over the old flower heads become woody and are often harvested for dried indoor decoration. The plant dies down completely during the winter. Height 24–36 inches (60–90cm).

CULTIVATION
Grow in a moist soil or up to 6 inches (15cm) of water in an open, sunny position. To prevent unwanted seeding, remove old flower stems as soon as the flowers have faded. Propagation is by division of the plants in spring, or from seed sown as soon as it ripens.

APONOGETON DISTACHYOS
(Water hawthorn)

MINIMUM TEMPERATURE **5°F (–15°C)**
ZONE **7**

CHARACTERISTICS
Submerged aquatic plant with floating foliage. The leaves are roughly rectangular with rounded ends and are dark olive green splashed sparingly with maroon or deep purple. The flowers, which are held just above the water, are forked and consist of two white bractlike organs with black stamens. They are produced throughout the summer and have a strong vanilla fragrance. Spread 18–24 inches (45–60cm).

CULTIVATION
Grow in between 12–36 inches (30–90cm) of water in a potting mix, ideally in a small aquatic planting basket, in full sun. Propagation is by division of established plants during early spring, or by using seed sown in pots of saturated heavy soil while they are still green.

ASTILBE x CRISPA 'PERKEA'

MINIMUM TEMPERATURE **–4°F (–20°C)**
ZONE **6**

CHARACTERISTICS
Very hardy dwarf, moisture-loving perennial with handsome, much-divided, bronze-green leaves. Feathery plumes of deep pink flowers are produced during mid- to late summer. A clump-forming plant that dies down completely for the winter months. Height 8 inches (20cm).

CULTIVATION
Grow in a moisture-retaining, richly organic soil in a sunny position. Although it will tolerate occasional inundation with water, it grows best in moist soil rather than in standing water. Remove the old flower spikes as soon as flowering finishes. Propagation is by division of the woody crowns during autumn or early spring.

AZOLLA CAROLINIANA
(Fairy moss)

MINIMUM TEMPERATURE **5°F (–15°C)**
ZONE **7**

CHARACTERISTICS
Spreading, floating fern with delicate, soft green foliage often with a purplish tinge. In bright sunshine and at the approach of autumn it often takes on a strong reddish hue. Being a true fern, azolla does not produce any flowers.

CULTIVATION
Grow in an open, sunny position, preferably in water that is slightly alkaline. A free-floating plant, this does not take severe weather well. As a precaution against winter loss in cold areas, remove a portion of the fronds toward the end of the growing season and place in a bowl of water with a little soil in the bottom in a light, frost-free place. This provides an early start again in the spring. Propagation is by separation and redistribution of groups of foliage.

BUTOMUS UMBELLATUS
(Flowering rush)

MINIMUM TEMPERATURE **–13°F (–25°C)**
ZONE **5**

CHARACTERISTICS
Very hardy, elegant, rushlike, marginal aquatic plant with narrow, bright green, slightly twisted foliage in neat clumps. Spreading, showy umbels of bright rose-pink flowers are produced during late summer. A white-flowered form is also available. The plant dies back and becomes completely dormant during the winter. Height 24–36 inches (60–90cm).

CULTIVATION
Grow in moist soil or up to 9 inches (23cm) of water in an open, sunny position. Remove the old flower stems as they fade. Knock waterlily aphids off with a strong stream of water from a hose. Propagation is by removing bulbils from the base of mature plants during early spring, or by division of established clumps in the growing season.

CALLA PALUSTRIS
(Bog arum)

MINIMUM TEMPERATURE **–22°F (–30°C)**
ZONE **4**

CHARACTERISTICS
A late spring- or early summer-flowering, marginal aquatic plant with small, white sail-like flowers that are replaced by bright orange-red fruits during late summer and early autumn. A scrambling plant, it produces strong, creeping stems that are densely clothed with bright green, glossy, heart-shaped leaves. Height 6–12 inches (15–30cm).

CULTIVATION
Grow in an open, sunny position in moist soil or up to 2 inches (5cm) of water. Plants soon become untidy and so should be lifted, have young growths separated out, and be replanted each spring. Propagation is either from seed sown as soon as it ripens, or from short sections of creeping stem, each with a bud, inserted in trays of saturated heavy soil.

CALTHA LEPTOSEPALA
(Mountain marigold)

MINIMUM TEMPERATURE **–31°F (–35°C)**
ZONE **3**

CHARACTERISTICS
Small-growing, marginal aquatic plant of neat habit producing a mound of dark green, scalloped foliage that is pleasing even when the plant is not in flower. Broad, white, saucer-shaped flowers are produced during late spring and early summer. The plant dies back completely for the winter months. Height 6–18 inches (15–45cm).

CULTIVATION
Grow in a sunny position in moist soil or up to 2 inches (5cm) of water. Remove faded flower heads. Lift and divide plants every second year in order to maintain vigor. Propagation is by division of plants after flowering, or by seed sown in pots of saturated heavy soil as soon as it ripens.

CALTHA PALUSTRIS
(Marsh marigold)

MINIMUM TEMPERATURE **–31°F (–35°C)**
ZONE **3**

CHARACTERISTICS

Lovely early-flowering, marginal aquatic plant. Very hardy, with neat, dark green mounds of scalloped foliage and bright golden-yellow waxy flowers. 'Alba' has smaller white flowers with yellow centers, 'Flore Pleno' has bright golden, fully double flowers on neater growing plants. It dies back completely during the winter months. Height 12–24 inches (30–60cm).

CULTIVATION

Grow in moist soil or up to 12 inches (30cm) of water in a sunny position. In summer, mildew and fungal infections may occur, disfiguring the foliage. Treat badly infested plants with an organic fungicide, and remove faded flowers and deteriorating leaves. Propagation is by division of established plants during spring, or from seed sown in pots of saturated heavy soil as soon as the seeds ripen.

CAREX ELATA 'BOWLES' GOLDEN' (syn. C. elata 'Aurea') (Golden tufted sedge)

MINIMUM TEMPERATURE **5°F (–15°C)**
ZONE **7**

CHARACTERISTICS

Most attractive bog garden sedge, with coarse, grassy, bright golden foliage with narrow green edges. Insignificant tufts of flowers during summer that are generally removed to preserve the quality of the foliage. Clump-forming, in mild winters remaining more or less evergreen. Height 16–24 inches (40–60cm).

CULTIVATION

Prefers an open, sunny position in damp soil. Does not enjoy standing in water during winter. The best golden color is produced when the soil is poor. A high level of nutrients tends to encourage pale green foliage. Propagation is by division of established plants during early spring.

CERATOPHYLLUM DEMERSUM
(Hornwort, Coontail)

MINIMUM TEMPERATURE **14°F (–10°C)**
ZONE **8**

CHARACTERISTICS

Totally submerged aquatic plant with whorls of dark green, needlelike, bristly foliage on slender, brittle stems. In early spring, these are sometimes temporarily rooted to the pool floor, but for most of the year are completely free-floating just beneath the surface of the water. In winter the plant disperses as turions or winter buds, reappearing when the water warms up again in the spring.

CULTIVATION

A most adaptable, submerged aquatic plant for full sun or partial shade. Although it is normally introduced to a water feature as a bunched plant, it rarely roots and is usually allowed to grow largely unrestricted beneath the water surface. Propagation is by separation and redistribution of the scrambling growths.

CYPERUS ISOCLADUS
(syn. C. 'Haspan')
(Miniature papyrus)

MINIMUM TEMPERATURE **32°F (0°C)**
ZONE **10**

CHARACTERISTICS
A miniature version of the famous Egyptian papyrus for small-pool cultivation indoors. An elegant plant with stout stems that give rise to umbrellalike heads of very fine, bright green foliage. Insignificant brownish flowers are produced. When grown under warm conditions of at least 59°F (15°C), it remains completely evergreen. Height 24–36 inches (60–90cm).

CULTIVATION
A marginal aquatic plant tolerating conditions from moist soil up to 6 inches (15cm) of water. It is happy in full sun or partial shade and is easily increased by division during the active growing season. It is best grown with a minimum night temperature of 59°F (15°C).

EGERIA DENSA
(syn. Elodea densa)

MINIMUM TEMPERATURE **23°F (–5°C)**
ZONE **9**

CHARACTERISTICS
Totally submerged aquatic plant of similar appearance to, and often confused with, the very hardy goldfish weed (*Lagarosiphon major*). Dark green, crispy leaflets are carried in dense whorls around strong, green, scrambling stems. The flowers are insignificant. A very popular plant for the fish hobbyist. Is reliably evergreen when maintained above freezing.

CULTIVATION
Ideally grow with a minimum water temperature of 50°F (10°C) in order to maintain a lush, well-clothed appearance. The clumps of plant should be rooted into a container on the floor of the water feature. Propagation is from short stem cuttings taken during the active growing season and fastened together with a twist tie. Bunches like this are then planted in their permanent positions.

ELEOCHARIS ACICULARIS
(Hairgrass, Needle spike-rush)

MINIMUM TEMPERATURE **5°F (–15°C)**
ZONE **7**

CHARACTERISTICS
Totally submerged aquatic plant that looks rather like a carpet of grass, although in no way is it related to that group of plants. It is a close relative of the rushes and sedges. An evergreen plant, even in freezing conditions, that produces bright green foliage. Height up to 8 inches (20cm).

CULTIVATION
The perfect submerged aquatic plant for tub or sink gardening, growing in a restrained clump-forming fashion. Although very hardy, it also responds well to tropical conditions. Propagation is by division of the clumps. Unlike most other submerged plants, cuttings will not root.

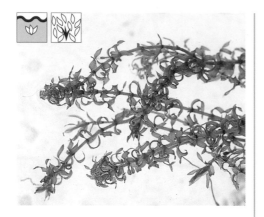

ELODEA CANADENSIS
(Canadian pondweed)

MINIMUM TEMPERATURE **-4°F (-20°C)**
ZONE **6**

CHARACTERISTICS
This handsome and widely cultivated aquatic remains completely submerged. Small, dark green leaves are arranged in very dense whorls along extensive branching stems. Unless the weather is very severe, elodea usually remains evergreen and is much enjoyed by the fish.

CULTIVATION
Although *Elodea canadensis* has a reputation for being invasive, it is easily contained if restricted to a planter. Although evergreen, it should ideally be replaced with fresh cuttings from early spring growth each year. These should be gathered together and secured with a twist tie before planting. This is also the method for propagation.

HOSTA FORTUNEI 'GOLD STANDARD'

MINIMUM TEMPERATURE **-4°F (-20°C)**
ZONE **6**

CHARACTERISTICS
Perennial bog plant with heavily textured, golden, rounded leaves edged with dark green. Although grown primarily as a foliage plant, it produces spikes of pendent, pale lavender bell-like flowers during midsummer. Hostas die back at the first sign of frost, disappearing completely for the winter. Height 16–24 inches (40–60cm).

CULTIVATION
Grow in a wet, richly organic soil, but not in standing water, in either sun or partial shade. Protect from attacks by slugs early in the growing season. Propagation is by division of established clumps during early spring. At this time, if carefully lifted with a fork, the clump should separate easily.

HOSTA PLANTAGINEA
(August lily)

MINIMUM TEMPERATURE **-4°F (-20°C)**
ZONE **6**

CHARACTERISTICS
Perennial bog plant with glossy green leaves with conspicuous veins, and wavy margins. Although grown primarily as a foliage plant, it produces spikes of fragrant pendent white tubular flowers during midsummer. Hostas die back at the first sign of frost, disappearing completely for the winter. Height 16–24 inches (40–60cm).

CULTIVATION
Grow in a wet, richly organic soil, but not in standing water, in sun or partial shade. Protect from attacks by slugs early in the growing season. Propagation is by division of established clumps during early spring. At this time, lift carefully with a fork and the plants will separate easily.

HOSTA SIEBOLDIANA 'ELEGANS'

MINIMUM TEMPERATURE **–4°F (–20°C)**
ZONE **6**

CHARACTERISTICS
Perennial bog plant with beautiful steely-blue, oval leaves with a ribbed and corrugated surface. Although grown primarily as a foliage plant, it produces strong spikes of handsome, pale lilac or slightly-off-white tubular flowers during midsummer. Hostas die back at the first sign of frost, disappearing completely for the winter. Height 16–24 inches (40–60cm).

CULTIVATION
Grow in a wet, richly organic soil, but not in standing water, in sun or partial shade. Protect from attacks by slugs early in the growing season. Propagation is by division of established clumps during early spring. At this time, lift carefully with a fork and the plants will separate easily.

HOSTA SIEBOLDIANA 'FRANCES WILLIAMS'

MINIMUM TEMPERATURE **–4°F (–20°C)**
ZONE **6**

CHARACTERISTICS
Perennial bog plant with beautiful blue-green, ribbed leaves with a beige edge. Although grown primarily as a foliage plant, it produces strong spikes of pendent, pale lilac or off-white tubular flowers during midsummer. Hostas die back at the first sign of frost, disappearing completely for the winter. Height 16–24 inches (40–60cm).

CULTIVATION
Grow in a wet, richly organic soil, but not in standing water, in either sun or partial shade. Protect from attacks by slugs early in the growing season. Propagation is by division of established clumps during early spring. At this time, if carefully lifted with a fork, the clump should separate easily.

HOSTA 'THOMAS HOGG'

MINIMUM TEMPERATURE **–4°F (–20°C)**
ZONE **6**

CHARACTERISTICS
Perennial bog plant with large, bold, green leaves with a distinctive white margin. Although grown primarily as a foliage plant, it produces spikes of slender, pendent, lilac tubular flowers during midsummer. Hostas die back at the first sign of frost, disappearing completely for the winter. Height 10–16 inches (25–40cm).

CULTIVATION
Grow in a wet, richly organic soil, but not in standing water, in either sun or partial shade. Protect from attacks by slugs early in the growing season. Propagation is by division of established clumps during early spring. At this time, if carefully lifted with a fork, the clump should separate easily.

HOSTA UNDULATA 'MEDIO-VARIEGATA'

MINIMUM TEMPERATURE **-4°F (-20°C)**
ZONE **6**

CHARACTERISTICS
Perennial bog plant with undulating, lance-shaped, cream-and-green variegated leaves. Although grown primarily as a foliage plant, it produces narrow spikes of slender, pendent, lilac bell-like flowers during midsummer. Hostas die back at the first sign of frost, disappearing completely for the winter. Height 10–16 inches (25–40cm).

CULTIVATION
Grow in a wet, richly organic soil, but not in standing water, in either sun or partial shade. Protect from attacks by slugs early in the growing season. Propagation is by division of established clumps during early spring. At this time, if carefully lifted with a fork, the clump should separate easily.

HOSTA VENTRICOSA

MINIMUM TEMPERATURE **-4°F (-20°C)**
ZONE **6**

CHARACTERISTICS
Perennial bog plant with narrow and slightly undulating, bright green leaves. Although grown primarily as a foliage plant, it produces spikes of attractive, pendent, deep lilac-mauve tubular flowers during midsummer. Hostas die back at the first sign of frost, disappearing completely for the winter. Height 12–20 inches (30–50cm).

CULTIVATION
Grow in a wet, richly organic soil, but not in standing water, in either sun or partial shade. Protect from attacks by slugs early in the growing season. Propagation is by division of established clumps during early spring. At this time, if carefully lifted with a fork, the clump should separate easily.

HOUTTUYNIA CORDATA 'CHAMELEON'
(syn. H. cordata 'Variegata')

MINIMUM TEMPERATURE **-13°F (-25°C)**
ZONE **5**

CHARACTERISTICS
Marginal or bog garden perennial with beautiful yellow, red, purple, and green variegated foliage. Although hardy to zone 5, this does require thoughtful placement as the young shoots are vulnerable to frost damage. The roughly heart-shaped leaves have an unpleasant odor if bruised. Small, creamy white cone-shaped flowers are produced sparingly during the summer. The whole plant dies down completely for the winter. Height 6–12 inches (15–30cm).

CULTIVATION
Choose a moist soil in a sunny position. Although houttuynias will grow in up to 2 inches (5cm) of water, they make the most orderly plants when grown in wet soil. Propagation is by division once the plants reemerge in the spring.

HOUTTUYNIA CORDATA 'FLORE PLENO'

MINIMUM TEMPERATURE **–13°F (–25°C)**
ZONE **5**

CHARACTERISTICS
Marginal or bog garden perennial with roughly heart-shaped, bluish-green foliage flushed with purple. The leaves have an unpleasant odor if bruised. The prominent, fully double, creamy, conelike flowers have an attractive ruff of petals. Height 6–12 inches (15–30cm).

CULTIVATION
Although capable of growing in standing water, it is much better treated as a moisture-loving plant and grown in damp, richly organic soil. Place carefully, for although fully hardy it is very vulnerable to frost damage to the shoots during early spring. Propagation is by division once the plants reemerge in the spring.

HYDROCHARIS MORSUS-RANAE
(Frogbit)

MINIMUM TEMPERATURE **–22°F (–30°C)**
ZONE **4**

CHARACTERISTICS
Hardy, small, floating plant that looks rather like a tiny waterlily. The three-petaled white flowers with a yellow center are delicate and papery and appear freely during the summer months. As winter approaches frogbit produces turions or winter buds that fall to the bottom of the pool, reappearing again during spring when the water warms up.

CULTIVATION
Free-floating, these prosper in a warm, sunny, open position. At the approach of winter, turions can be collected and overwintered in a bowl of water with a little soil in the bottom in a frost-free, light environment in order to encourage early growth. Propagation is by separation and redistribution of the plantlets during the summer.

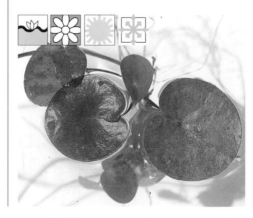

IRIS ENSATA
(*syn. I. kaempferi*)
(Japanese clematis-flowered iris/flag)

MINIMUM TEMPERATURE **–4°F (–20°C)**
ZONE **6**

CHARACTERISTICS
One of the most outstanding irises for the bog garden. Produces tufts of broad, grassy or narrow, swordlike foliage with expansive, velvety, deep purple flowers during summer. There are many fine cultivars, including 'Queen of the Blues', soft purplish-pink 'Pink Frost', rich yellow 'Gold Bound', and the bold violet-blue flowered 'Variegata' with striking cream-and-green-striped foliage. Height 24–30 inches (60–75cm).

CULTIVATION
All cultivars of *I. ensata* dislike alkalinity, so it is important to mix plenty of peat into the growing medium. Summer inundation with water presents no problems, but during the winter these iris must be kept just moist. Remove faded flower heads. Propagation is by division just after flowering.

IRIS LAEVIGATA
(Asiatic water iris)

MINIMUM TEMPERATURE **–4°F (–20°C)**
ZONE **6**

CHARACTERISTICS
An easily grown, hardy, marginal aquatic plant, forming clumps of smooth, sword-shaped green leaves. Beautiful blue flowers during midsummer. There are many named cultivars to choose from, including the deep purple-blue and white 'Colchesteri', soft pink 'Rose Queen', pure white 'Snowdrift', and the blue-flowered variegated-leafed 'Variegata'. Height 24–36 inches (60–90cm).

CULTIVATION
Grow in an open, sunny position in up to 4 inches (10cm) of water in any heavy growing medium. Propagation is by division of established clumps immediately after flowering.

IRIS SIBIRICA
(Siberian iris)

MINIMUM TEMPERATURE **–22°F (–30°C)**
ZONE **4**

CHARACTERISTICS
Excellent, very hardy bog garden plant with vigorous tufts of slender grassy foliage from which emerge elegant, pale blue flowers, several to a slender stem. There are many cultivars including the white and creamy yellow 'Butter and Sugar', dark purple-blue 'Caesar's Brother', the dwarf blue-flowered 'Perry's Pygmy', and rich blue 'Super Ego'. There is also a short-growing white-flowered kind called 'Little White'. All flower during midsummer. Height 18–36 inches (45–90cm).

CULTIVATION
Grow in an open, sunny position in moist soil. After flowering remove the faded flower heads. Propagation is by division of established clumps of plants as soon as flowering is over.

IRIS VERSICOLOR
(Blue flag)

MINIMUM TEMPERATURE **–13°F (–25°C)**
ZONE **5**

CHARACTERISTICS
A first-class, marginal plant of compact growth with plain green swordlike leaves. The flowers are produced during midsummer and are violet-blue and purple conspicuously marked with creamy yellow. The most widely grown cultivar is the rich plum-colored 'Kermesina'. Height 18–24 inches (45–60cm).

CULTIVATION
Grow in an open, sunny position in up to 4 inches (10cm) of water in any heavy growing medium. Propagation is by division of established clumps immediately after flowering. The species can also be increased from seed sown in trays of saturated, heavy soil in the spring.

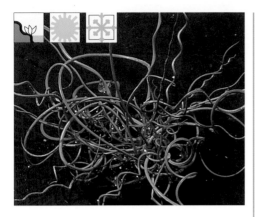

JUNCUS EFFUSUS 'SPIRALIS'
(Corkscrew rush)

MINIMUM TEMPERATURE **–22°F (–30°C)**
ZONE **4**

CHARACTERISTICS
A most curious, hardy marginal plant with soft, dark green, needlelike leaves that are twisted and contorted like a corkscrew. During summer it produces strange, small, brownish flowers of little merit. Grown for its strange contorted stems. Height 12–18 inches (30–45cm).

CULTIVATION
Grow in any open, sunny position in up to 2 inches (5cm) of water. Any straight stems that are produced should be removed as soon as visible in order to prevent them from swamping the desirable contorted growths. Propagation is by division of established plants in the spring. Take care to use only twisted growths when replanting.

LAGAROSIPHON MAJOR
(syn. *Elodea crispa*)
(Goldfish weed)

MINIMUM TEMPERATURE **–22°F (–30°C)**
ZONE **4**

CHARACTERISTICS
Totally submerged, hardy aquatic plant with long, dark green succulent stems and dark green, crispy foliage. The summer flowers are minute and insignificant. Except in very low temperatures, almost always evergreen.

CULTIVATION
Grow completely submerged in a sunny position. Replace each spring with short stem cuttings bunched together with a heavy weight in order to maintain health and vigor. Propagation is from cuttings taken during the active growing season.

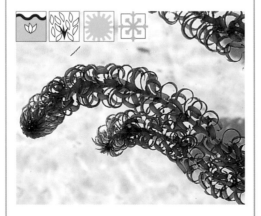

LOBELIA CARDINALIS 'COMPLIMENT SCARLET'

MINIMUM TEMPERATURE **–31°F (–35°C)**
ZONE **3**

CHARACTERISTICS
Moisture-loving perennial for boggy ground, with spires of bright red flowers during late summer above groups of soft green foliage. Dies down to overwintering rosettes of foliage in autumn. Height 30–36 inches (75–90cm).

CULTIVATION
Grow in an open, sunny position in wet soil. The plant will tolerate standing in a little water during summer, but will die out in the winter if in anything other than damp soil. Although hardy to zone 3, some gardeners prefer to lift one or two rosettes of overwintering foliage and place them in slightly drier conditions in a cold frame. Propagation is by autumn or spring division, or from seed sown in a greenhouse very early in the year.

LOBELIA x GERARDII 'VEDRARIENSIS'

MINIMUM TEMPERATURE **–22°F (–30°C)**
ZONE **4**

CHARACTERISTICS
A bold and easily grown moisture-loving perennial, with intense violet-purple flowers during late summer. The leaves are pale green with a strong purple infusion. Dies down to overwintering rosettes of foliage in autumn. Height 30–36 inches (75–90cm).

CULTIVATION
Grow in moist soil in a sunny position. This lobelia will not tolerate standing water at any time. Propagation is by division of the overwintering rosettes of foliage either in autumn or early spring. It is also easily raised from seed sown during spring in a cold frame.

LOBELIA x SPECIOSA 'QUEEN VICTORIA'

MINIMUM TEMPERATURE **–22°F (–30°C)**
ZONE **4**

CHARACTERISTICS
Moisture-loving perennial, with very attractive red-purple-colored leaves and spires of bright scarlet blossoms during late summer. Dies down to overwintering rosettes of foliage in autumn. Height 30–36 inches (75–90cm).

CULTIVATION
Grow in an open, sunny position in wet soil. The plant will tolerate some standing water during summer, but will die out during winter if inundated. Although hardy to zone 4, it is a wise precaution to lift one or two rosettes of overwintering foliage and place in slightly drier conditions in a cold frame. Propagation is by division during autumn or early spring.

LOBELIA SPLENDENS (syn. Lobelia fulgens)

MINIMUM TEMPERATURE **14°F (–10°C)**
ZONE **8**

CHARACTERISTICS
Moisture-loving perennial, with purplish-green or purple leaves and large spires of scarlet flowers during late summer. A very variable, but nonetheless beautiful, plant that dies back during autumn to overwintering rosettes of foliage. Height 12–24 inches (30–60cm).

CULTIVATION
Grow in a moist position, preferably in full sun. This lobelia does not enjoy standing water at any time. It can survive quite cold conditions if frozen constantly, but it is recommended to lift several overwintering rosettes of foliage in autumn and to keep them in a cold frame as a precaution against winter demise. Propagation is by autumn or spring division, or by using seed sown in a greenhouse during early spring.

LOBELIA SYPHILITICA

MINIMUM TEMPERATURE **–31°F (–35°C)**
ZONE **3**

CHARACTERISTICS
Very hardy perennial for wet, boggy
conditions. Spires of blue, or very
occasionally white, flowers are produced
above rather coarse, plain green foliage
during summer. Dies down during
autumn to overwintering rosettes of
foliage. Height 12–24 inches (30–60cm).

CULTIVATION
Grow in full sun or partial shade in moist
soil. This lobelia will not tolerate
standing water at any time of the year.
Propagation by division of the
overwintering rosettes during spring.
Seed can also be sown in spring in a cold
frame, but the resulting plants will show
variation in flower color and stature.

LYSIMACHIA NUMMULARIA
(Creeping Jenny)

MINIMUM TEMPERATURE **–22°F (–30°C)**
ZONE **4**

CHARACTERISTICS
An easygoing and very hardy, more or
less evergreen carpeting plant for very
wet places, even growing submerged
when given the opportunity. Throughout
much of the summer the foliage is
studded with bright golden-yellow
buttercuplike flowers. There is a beautiful
golden-leafed cultivar called 'Aurea' that
also has yellow flowers. Height 2 inches
(5cm).

CULTIVATION
This plant is extremely tolerant of both
soil and situation, prospering in sun or
shade in moist soil or standing water. A
quite vigorous grower, it benefits from
being replaced every second year with
fresh cuttings. These root easily in a
mixture of equal parts peat and sharp
sand at any time from late spring until
late summer.

MATTEUCCIA
STRUTHIOPTERIS
(*syn. Struthiopteris germanica*)
(Ostrich fern)

MINIMUM TEMPERATURE **–40°F (–40°C)**
ZONE **2**

CHARACTERISTICS
The most beautiful, hardy, bog garden
fern. A large shuttlecock of lacy green
foliage is produced around a strong basal
crown. Although a very hardy plant, at
the first hint of frost the fronds turn a
coppery color and die back. During
winter it dies back to the ground
completely. Height 24–36 inches
(60–90cm).

CULTIVATION
A very versatile fern growing in moist
soil or several inches (10–15cm) of water
in either full sun or partial shade.
Propagation is by division of the creeping
rootstock during early spring, each piece
of creeping rhizome with a green
knucklelike shoot being capable of
growing into a mature fern.

MENTHA AQUATICA
(Water mint)

MINIMUM TEMPERATURE **–4°F (–20°C)**
ZONE **6**

CHARACTERISTICS
A strongly aromatic, hardy perennial plant with typical mintlike foliage. The leaves are dull green, rather downy, and borne on slender purple or reddish stems. During summer it produces whorls of soft lilac-pink or pink flowers that are loved by bees. Height 8–18 inches (20–45cm).

CULTIVATION
A vigorously growing plant that prospers in full sun or partial shade in moist soil or several inches (10–15cm) of water. It is easily propagated from short stem cuttings taken during summer, these being used to replace regularly older plants that have become woody and untidy.

MIMULUS x HYBRIDUS 'CALYPSO'

MINIMUM TEMPERATURE **14°F (–10°C)**
ZONE **8**

CHARACTERISTICS
Beautiful, exotic-looking, moisture-loving plants with burgundy, red, and yellow flowers that are produced throughout the summer. The flowers are flared and look rather like tropical orchids. The foliage is soft green and rounded forming neat hummocks. The plants die back in the autumn to overwintering rosettes. Height 6–8 inches (15–20cm).

CULTIVATION
Grow in moist soil, although tolerant of a little standing water during the summer months. Although perennial, it is not long-lived and sometimes dies out during the winter. Propagation is by spring division of overwintered rosettes, or from seed sown in a greenhouse in the spring.

MIMULUS x HYBRIDUS 'MALIBU'

MINIMUM TEMPERATURE **14°F (–10°C)**
ZONE **8**

CHARACTERISTICS
Bright orange-flowered hybrid musk with soft green leaves produced in neat mounds. The large, exotic flowers appear throughout much of the summer. The plants die back to overwintering rosettes in autumn. Height 10 inches (25cm).

CULTIVATION
Grow in moist soil, although tolerant of a little standing water during the summer months. Although perennial, it is not long-lived and sometimes dies out during the winter months. Propagation is from seed sown during the spring in a greenhouse, or by spring division of overwintered rosettes.

MIMULUS x HYBRIDUS 'QUEEN'S PRIZE'

MINIMUM TEMPERATURE **14°F (–10°C)**
ZONE **8**

CHARACTERISTICS

A large-flowered, but short-growing, strain of hybrid musk. It has beautiful, exotic-looking flowers in myriad colors from cream to red, variously spotted and stained with black, maroon, or white, and low-growing hummocks of soft green leaves. The plants die down to overwintering rosettes in autumn. Height 6 inches (15cm).

CULTIVATION

Grow in moist soil, although tolerant of a little standing water during the summer months. Although perennial, it is not long-lived and sometimes dies out during the winter months. Propagation is from seed sown in a greenhouse during the spring, or by spring division of overwintered rosettes.

MIMULUS LUTEUS
(Yellow musk)

MINIMUM TEMPERATURE **5°F (–15°C)**
ZONE **7**

CHARACTERISTICS

Free-flowering plant for moist soil or up to 6 inches (15cm) of water. Soft green, rounded foliage is freely produced on a vigorously growing and spreading plant. Spires of bright yellow tubular flowers produce a summer-long display. In autumn it dies back to overwintering rosettes of foliage. Height 18–24 inches (45–60cm).

CULTIVATION

Tolerates a little shade, but is much the best in full sun in either damp soil or up to 6 inches (15cm) of water. Remove faded flower heads regularly or they will self-seed freely and become a nuisance. Propagation is by spring division of the overwintered rosettes of foliage or using seed sown at any time during the spring and summer.

MIMULUS RINGENS
(Allegheny monkey flower)

MINIMUM TEMPERATURE **–31°F (–35°C)**
ZONE **3**

CHARACTERISTICS

A branching, slender, marginal plant with handsome, narrow, bright green leaves. The tubular soft lavender to blue flowers are produced freely on upright spiky stems. During winter the plant dies back completely. Height 16–18 inches (40–45cm).

CULTIVATION

Grows in either damp soil or up to 6 inches (15cm) of water. It prefers full sun, but can tolerate a little shade. Remove faded flower stems to encourage regrowth and often a second smaller flush of flowers. Easily propagated by spring division, or from seed sown in a greenhouse during spring or early summer.

MYRIOPHYLLUM AQUATICUM
(*syn. M. proserpinacoides*)
(Parrot feather)

MINIMUM TEMPERATURE **23°F (–5°C)**
ZONE **9**

CHARACTERISTICS
A totally, or sometimes partially, submerged aquatic plant with beautiful feathery foliage. Blue-green, finely cut leaves are produced on scrambling stems. When grown with the foliage above the water it often turns red or orange after the first touch of frost. Not reliably hardy and often grown as a greenhouse plant.

CULTIVATION
Although it can be grown totally submerged, this myriophyllum is best treated as a marginal plant and cultivated in a few inches (10–15cm) of water. If grown outside, take a few short stem cuttings during late summer for overwintering. Propagation is by removing short stem cuttings, bunching them together with a twist tie, and rooting in a pot of saturated, heavy soil.

MYRIOPHYLLUM SPICATUM
(Spiked water milfoil)

MINIMUM TEMPERATURE **–4°F (–20°C)**
ZONE **6**

CHARACTERISTICS
Totally submerged aquatic plant with small red and yellowish flower spikes that appear above the surface of the water during summer. The finely divided, filigree foliage is bronze-green and produced in dense masses on strong, twining, succulent stems. A vigorous plant much loved by fish. Dies back during winter.

CULTIVATION
Grow totally submerged in up to 36 inches (90cm) of water. A first-class oxygenating plant that requires plenty of light. Propagation is by short stem cuttings taken during the spring and summer, fastened together with a twist tie, and rooted in saturated, heavy soil.

MYRIOPHYLLUM VERTICILLATUM

MINIMUM TEMPERATURE **–31°F (–35°C)**
ZONE **3**

CHARACTERISTICS
Completely submerged, very hardy aquatic plant with elegant, fine, dark green filigree foliage and insignificant flowers during the summer. A vigorous plant much utilized by fish fanciers. In winter it dies back almost completely. Very similar to M. *spicatum*, but much more resilient.

CULTIVATION
Grow totally submerged in up to 36 inches (90cm) of water. An excellent oxygenating plant demanding an open situation with plenty of light. Propagation is from short stem cuttings taken during spring and summer, fastened together with a twist tie, and rooted in saturated, heavy soil. Benefits from regular replacement.

NYMPHAEA 'AURORA'

MINIMUM TEMPERATURE **−4°F (−20°C)**
ZONE **6**

CHARACTERISTICS
Beautiful small-growing waterlily, with attractive purplish and green mottled leaves and handsome flowers that change color with each passing day. Popularly referred to as a chameleon or changeable waterlily, this starts off with a cream bud that opens to a yellow flower that then passes through orange shades to blood red. As the change takes place over several days, a number of different flowers are out at the same time. Spread 12–24 inches (30–60cm).

CULTIVATION
Grow in up to 18 inches (45cm) of water in a heavy potting mix. Lift and divide every three or four years. Propagation is by spring division or by the rooting of the eyes, which appear with varying frequency on the tuberous rootstock.

NYMPHAEA CAERULEA
(Blue lotus)

MINIMUM TEMPERATURE **34°F (1°C)**
ZONE **10**

CHARACTERISTICS
Tropical waterlily, with starlike soft blue flowers held above the surface of the water. Round, fresh green, floating foliage spotted with purple and black. Dies down completely for the winter. Spread 18–38 inches (45–95cm).

CULTIVATION
Grow in a greenhouse or outdoors in a sunny position where there is a consistent temperature of 75°F (24°C). Requires a richly organic compost. Plant in a container and cover the surface with a layer of fine gravel. Store overwintering tubers in trays of damp sand in a frost-free place. Propagation is by separating out the tubers during the autumn or by dividing plants in the spring once they have started into growth.

NYMPHAEA 'GRAZIELLA'

MINIMUM TEMPERATURE **−4°F (−20°C)**
ZONE **6**

CHARACTERISTICS
The perfect small-growing waterlily for tub culture. Orange-red flowers up to 2 inches (5cm) across with deep orange stamens produced for most of the summer. Olive-green leaves splashed and spotted with brown and purple. Dies back completely during winter. Spread 12–30 inches (30–75cm).

CULTIVATION
Grow in a potting mix in an open, sunny position in up to 24 inches (60cm) of water. Lift and divide every third year. Propagation is by spring division or by rooting the sprouts or eyes that appear clustered around the rootstock of the plant.

NYMPHAEA 'LAYDEKERI ALBA'

MINIMUM TEMPERATURE **–4°F (–20°C)**
ZONE **6**

CHARACTERISTICS
An excellent, small-growing waterlily with starlike, pure white flowers up to 4 inches (10cm) across that have a distinctive aroma of a freshly opened packet of tea. The dark green leaves have a purplish flush beneath. Dies down completely during the winter months. Spread 12–24 inches (30–60cm).

CULTIVATION
Grow in a potting mix, ideally in a proper aquatic planting container in an open, sunny position in up to 24 inches (60cm) of water. Lift and divide in the spring every three or four years. Propagation is by spring division of established plants or by the rooting of sprouts or eyes that appear at varying intervals along the woody rootstock.

NYMPHAEA 'LAYDEKERI FULGENS'

MINIMUM TEMPERATURE **–4°F (–20°C)**
ZONE **6**

CHARACTERISTICS
A small-growing waterlily, with starlike, fragrant, bright crimson flowers with reddish stamens. The dark green leaves have purplish undersides and a distinctive brown speckling around the leaf stalk. Dies down completely for the winter months. Spread 12–24 inches (30–60cm).

CULTIVATION
Grow in a potting mix, ideally in a proper aquatic planting container in an open, sunny position in up to 24 inches (60cm) of water. Lift and divide in the spring every three or four years. Propagation is by spring division of established plants or by the rooting of sprouts or eyes that appear at varying intervals along the woody rootstock.

NYMPHAEA TETRAGONA 'ALBA'
(syn. *N. pygmaea* 'Alba')
(Pygmy white waterlily)

MINIMUM TEMPERATURE **–4°F (–20°C)**
ZONE **6**

CHARACTERISTICS
The perfect small waterlily for sink garden or small tub. Tiny, papery, white flowers scarcely 1 inch (2.5cm) across are produced among small, oval, dark green leaves with purple undersides. Dies down completely during the winter. Spread 12–18 inches (30–45cm).

CULTIVATION
Grow in a potting mix in an open, sunny position in up to 12 inches (30cm) of water. Lift and replant every two or three years. Propagation is by seed only as the plant does not produce eyes or divisions. Sow seed in trays of saturated, heavy soil covered by ⅜ inch (1cm) of water in a greenhouse as soon as it ripens. Prick out the seedlings individually into small pots.

NYMPHAEA TETRAGONA 'HELVOLA'
(syn. N. pygmaea 'Helvola')

MINIMUM TEMPERATURE **–4°F (–20°C)**
ZONE **6**

CHARACTERISTICS
Very free-flowering, pygmy yellow waterlily. It has beautiful starlike flowers held just above deep olive-green leaves that are liberally splashed and stained with purple and brown. Dies down completely during the winter. Spread 12–18 inches (30–45cm).

CULTIVATION
Grow in a potting mix in an open, sunny position in up to 12 inches (30cm) of water. Lift and divide in the spring every third season. Propagation is by spring division or by the rooting of young growths or eyes from around the base of the rootstock.

NYMPHAEA TETRAGONA 'RUBRA'
(syn. N. pygmaea 'Rubra')

MINIMUM TEMPERATURE **–4°F (–20°C)**
ZONE **6**

CHARACTERISTICS
Tiny, blood-red, starlike flowers with orange-red stamens produced among dark olive-green leaves with a strong purplish cast. The kidney-shaped leaves have distinctive reddish undersides. Dies down completely during the winter. Spread 12–18 inches (30–45cm).

CULTIVATION
Grow in a potting mix in an open, sunny position in up to 12 inches (30cm) of water. Not being a vigorous grower, this waterlily can be successfully cultivated in a large bucket. Lift and divide in the spring every four or five years. Propagation is by occasional division or by the removal and rooting of young growths or eyes from the main rootstock, although these are sparingly produced.

ONOCLEA SENSIBILIS
(Sensitive fern)

MINIMUM TEMPERATURE **–22°F (–30°C)**
ZONE **4**

CHARACTERISTICS
Very beautiful, moisture-loving fern with deeply cut, erect, flattened fronds with a rose-pink spring flush. They eventually turn to a soft lime-green hue and by midsummer are mid-green. At the first touch of frost the fronds wither and die back so that there is nothing to be seen during the winter. Height 18–24 inches (45–60cm).

CULTIVATION
Grow in wet soil or with just a covering of water. Remove faded fronds in the autumn. Propagation is by division of the creeping rootstock during early spring just as the fronds appear.

PISTIA STRATIOTES
(Water lettuce)

MINIMUM TEMPERATURE **34°F (1°C)**
ZONE **10**

CHARACTERISTICS
Tropical free-floating plant, with bold rosettes of soft green, strongly ribbed, downy foliage. Surprisingly a member of the arum family, it produces tiny green insignificant flowers among its leaves. Its general appearance is of a rather fleshy floating lettuce.

CULTIVATION
Free-floating and generally requiring a consistent temperature of around 75°F (24°C) in order to prosper, it will also survive at lower temperatures. Prefers a little shade, although it will grow well in full sun. Take care not to splash the downy foliage with water or else it will suffer from sun scorch. Propagation is by division and separation of the young plants.

PLEIOBLASTUS PYGMAEUS
(syn. *Arundinaria pygmaea*)
(Dwarf bamboo)

MINIMUM TEMPERATURE **14°F (–10°C)**
ZONE **6**

CHARACTERISTICS
Dwarf-growing, finely cut, leafy bamboo with mealy white stems. The mid-green foliage is slightly downy, often with a whitish powdery edge. An evergreen structural plant for a damp position. Height 6–12 inches (15–30cm).

CULTIVATION
Grow in damp soil in an open, sunny position. As stems and foliage fade remove from the base. Although hardy to zone 6, this bamboo is often used for decorative purposes indoors. It grows equally well in the house or greenhouse as in the garden. Propagation is by careful division in late spring, outer portions of the plant being used to grow on.

PONTEDERIA CORDATA
(Pickerel weed)

MINIMUM TEMPERATURE **–31°F (–35°C)**
ZONE **3**

CHARACTERISTICS
A stately, marginal aquatic plant that produces handsome, glossy green, lance-shaped foliage and strong spikes of soft blue flowers from mid- to late summer. There are also white and pale pink forms available. Dies back completely during the winter months. Height 24–36 inches (60–90cm).

CULTIVATION
Grow in moist soil or up to 6 inches (15cm) of water in an open, sunny position. Lift and divide in the spring every third year. Propagation is by spring division or by sowing seed, while still green, in trays of saturated, heavy soil during late summer. The emerging seedlings should be potted individually.

POTAMOGETON CRISPUS
(Curled pondweed)

MINIMUM TEMPERATURE **–4°F (–20°C)**
ZONE **6**

CHARACTERISTICS
One of the most beautiful, totally
submerged aquatic plants with bronze-
green translucent foliage not unlike that
of a seaweed. The leaves are crispy and
crimped and produced on extensive
scrambling succulent stems. In
midsummer small, insignificant red
flowers are produced just above the
surface of the water. Dies back to just a
few stems during the winter.

CULTIVATION
Grow completely submerged in an open,
sunny position. Propagation is from short
stem cuttings that are removed during
spring or early summer, bunched together
with a twist tie, and rooted in pots of
saturated, heavy soil. Replace the plants
completely at least every second year.

PRIMULA BEESIANA

MINIMUM TEMPERATURE **–4°F (–20°C)**
ZONE **6**

CHARACTERISTICS
Moisture-loving, hardy perennial bog
garden plant with bold green, heavily
textured foliage, during late spring and
early summer producing strong flower
stems with three or more dense whorls of
flowers. The flowers are a rosy carmine in
color and each has a distinctive yellow
eye. The plants die back completely
during the winter months. Height 24–30
inches (60–75cm).

CULTIVATION
Grow in full sun or partial shade in a
damp, richly organic soil. After flowering,
remove the old flower heads to prevent
self-seeding. Every three or four years lift,
divide, and replant, ideally as soon as
flowering is over. Propagation is from seed
sown in a cold frame as soon as it ripens.
Seed that is kept for spring sowing will
usually require freezing for about three
weeks in order to break its dormancy.

PRIMULA BULLEYANA

MINIMUM TEMPERATURE **–4°F (–20°C)**
ZONE **6**

CHARACTERISTICS
Moisture-loving, hardy perennial bog
garden plant with strong, heavily
textured mid-green foliage. During late
spring and early summer it produces
tiered whorls of bright orange flowers.
The plants die back completely during
the winter months. Height 24–30 inches
(60–75cm).

CULTIVATION
Grow in full sun or partial shade in a
damp, richly organic soil. After flowering,
remove the old flower heads to prevent
self-seeding. Every three or four years lift,
divide, and replant, ideally as soon as
flowering is over. Propagation is from seed
sown in a cold frame as soon as it ripens.
Seed that is kept for spring sowing will
usually require freezing for about three
weeks in order to break its dormancy.

PRIMULA DENTICULATA
(Drumstick primula)

MINIMUM TEMPERATURE **-4°F (-20°C)**
ZONE **6**

CHARACTERISTICS
A well-known primula that is often grown
in the mixed border. Large globular heads
of lilac, pink, purple, or white flowers are
borne on stout stems. The leaves are green,
large, and coarse, with a distinctive aroma
and often smothered beneath with a white
meal that also extends up the flower stems.
Dies back completely during the winter.
Height 12–24 inches (30–60cm).

CULTIVATION
Grow in full sun or partial shade in a
damp, richly organic soil. After
flowering, remove the old flower heads to
prevent self-seeding. Every three or four
years lift, divide, and replant as soon as
flowering is over. Propagation is from
seed sown in a cold frame as soon as it
ripens. Seed kept for spring sowing will
usually require freezing for about three
weeks in order to break its dormancy.

PRIMULA JAPONICA

MINIMUM TEMPERATURE **5°F (-15°C)**
ZONE **7**

CHARACTERISTICS
Summer-flowering, moisture-loving,
hardy perennial with bold candelabra
heads of deep red flowers on very strong
stems. These are produced from among
clumps of light green cabbagy leaves.
'Miller's Crimson' is a cultivar with even
more intense crimson flowers. Dies back
completely during the winter months.
Height 18–30 inches (45–75cm).

CULTIVATION
Grow in full sun or partial shade in a
damp, richly organic soil. When flowering
is over remove the old flower heads to
prevent self-seeding. Every three or four
years lift, divide, and replant as soon as
flowering is over. Propagation is from seed
sown in a cold frame as soon as it ripens.
Seed that is kept for spring sowing will
usually require freezing for about three
weeks in order to break its dormancy.

PRIMULA ROSEA

MINIMUM TEMPERATURE **-4°F (-20°C)**
ZONE **6**

CHARACTERISTICS
Short-growing, early spring-flowering
perennial bog garden plant with bright
rose-pink to red flowers, each with a
prominent yellow eye. These are
produced among the emerging soft green
leaves that in early spring have a strong
pinkish or purplish flush. Dies back
completely for the winter months.
Height 6–8 inches (15–20cm).

CULTIVATION
Grow in full sun or with a little shade in
a damp, richly organic soil. Every three
or four years lift, divide, and replant,
ideally as soon as flowering is over.
Propagation is from seed sown in a cold
frame as soon as it ripens. Seed that is
kept for spring sowing will usually require
freezing for about three weeks in order to
break its dormancy.

PRIMULA SIKKIMENSIS

MINIMUM TEMPERATURE **–4°F (–20°C)**
ZONE **6**

CHARACTERISTICS
Summer-flowering, moisture-loving, hardy perennial with bold green, heavily textured, rounded leaves with a strong and sweet aroma. Elegant heads of pendent funnel-shaped, fragrant, sulfur-yellow or creamy yellow flowers are produced on stout stems. Dies back completely during the winter months. Height 18–24 inches (45–60cm).

CULTIVATION
Grow in full sun or partial shade in a damp, richly organic soil. When flowering is over remove the old flower heads to prevent self-seeding. Every three or four years lift, divide, and replant as soon as flowering is over. Propagation is from seed sown in a cold frame as soon as it ripens. Seed that is kept for spring sowing will usually require freezing for about three weeks in order to break its dormancy.

PRIMULA VIALII
(Orchid primula)

MINIMUM TEMPERATURE **5°F (–15°C)**
ZONE **7**

CHARACTERISTICS
Exotic-looking, hardy perennial bog garden plant with lance-shaped leaves in neat basal tufts. From the center of each plant several short, stout stems protrude, ending in crowded heads of tubular, red and bluish-purple flowers. A most unusual primula that flowers during midsummer. Height 12–18 inches (30–45cm).

CULTIVATION
Grow in full sun or partial shade in a damp, richly organic soil. Remove old flower heads. Unlike most other primulas, this species often dies out naturally after flowering. If clumps persist for a number of years, division and replanting is desirable. Propagation is from seed sown in a cold frame as soon as it ripens. Seed that is kept for spring sowing will usually require freezing for about three weeks in order to break its dormancy.

SAGITTARIA LATIFOLIA
(Duck potato)

MINIMUM TEMPERATURE **5°F (–15°C)**
ZONE **7**

CHARACTERISTICS
Hardy, strong-growing, marginal aquatic producing neat clumps of bold, mid-green, arrow-shaped foliage and spikes of single, three-petaled, white flowers during summer. Dies down completely for the winter months and is often late emerging in the spring. Height 36–48 inches (90–120cm).

CULTIVATION
Grow in full sun in moist soil or up to 6 inches (15cm) of water. Knock waterlily aphids off with a strong stream of water from a hose. Lift and separate the overwintered tubers in spring. Propagation is by redistribution of the tubers.

SAGITTARIA SAGITTIFOLIA 'FLORE PLENO'
(Double arrowhead)

MINIMUM TEMPERATURE **5°F (–15°C)**
ZONE **7**

CHARACTERISTICS
Hardy, marginal aquatic plant with clumps of glossy, mid-green, arrow-shaped leaves and strong spikes of papery white, fully double flowers during summer. Dies down completely for the winter and is often late emerging in the spring. Height 12–18 inches (30–45cm).

CULTIVATION
Grow in full sun in moist soil or up to 6 inches (15cm) of water. Knock waterlily aphids off with a strong stream of water from a hose. Lift and separate the overwintered tubers in spring. Propagation is by redistribution of the tubers.

SISYRINCHIUM ANGUSTIFOLIUM
(Blue-eyed grass)

MINIMUM TEMPERATURE **–31°F (–35°C)**
ZONE **3**

CHARACTERISTICS
Small-growing, moisture-loving, perennial plant with very narrow grasslike leaves that are produced in tight clumps. Groups of between two and eight starlike or cup-shaped flowers of intense blue with yellow centers are produced on narrow winged stems among and above the foliage in summer. Height 6–16 inches (15–40cm).

CULTIVATION
Grow in moist soil in full sun. An open position is imperative if the flowers are to open. Although a perennial plant, it is not always long-lived and sometimes requires replacement after a couple of years. While it is possible to divide plants successfully in the spring, the more usual method of propagation is from seed sown as soon as it ripens or during early spring, preferably in a cold frame.

SISYRINCHIUM CALIFORNICUM var. BRACHYPUS
(syn. S. brachypus)
(Golden-eyed grass)

MINIMUM TEMPERATURE **14°F (–10°C)**
ZONE **8**

CHARACTERISTICS
Small-growing, moisture-loving, perennial plant with short swordlike, gray-green leaves growing in tight clumps. Groups of between two and five starlike bright yellow flowers are produced on narrow winged stems above the foliage during the summer. Height 6–10 inches (15–25cm).

CULTIVATION
Grow in moist soil in full sun. An open position is imperative if the flowers are to open. Although a perennial plant, it often behaves like an annual. While it is possible to divide any crowded plants that overwinter successfully in the spring, propagation is usually from seed sown as soon as it ripens or during early spring, preferably in a cold frame.

STRATIOTES ALOIDES
(Water soldier)

MINIMUM TEMPERATURE **–13°F (–25°C)**
ZONE **5**

CHARACTERISTICS
Hardy, free-floating, perennial aquatic plant that looks rather like a narrow-leafed pineapple top. It bears creamy white or pinkish papery flowers in the leaf axils. Male flowers appear in clusters, female flowers alone. Both are produced during the summer months. During winter the plant sinks to the floor of the pool.

CULTIVATION
Allow to free-float in an open, sunny position. The plant produces young plantlets from runners and these are used for propagation purposes, after being detached and redistributed.

TRAPA NATANS
(Water chestnut)

MINIMUM TEMPERATURE **–13°F (–25°C)**
ZONE **5**

CHARACTERISTICS
A handsome, free-floating aquatic with rosettes of dark green, rhomboidal leaves and attractive white axillary flowers. While behaving like a perennial, trapa is really an annual growing seasonally from spiny dark brown nuts that, at the approach of winter, come to rest on the floor of the pool. They reappear and germinate as the water begins to warm up.

CULTIVATION
Grow in a sunny position in open water. If left to their own devices, trapa nuts that have fallen to the pool floor will eventually germinate. Gather a few nuts in the autumn for overwintering purposes and place these in a frost-free place in a bowl of water with a little soil on the bottom. These will germinate much more speedily and provide early spring foliage.

TYPHA LATIFOLIA
(Greater reedmace, Cattail)

MINIMUM TEMPERATURE **–31°F (–35°C)**
ZONE **3**

CHARACTERISTICS
Strong-growing, hardy, perennial marginal aquatic plant, with tall, broad, gray-green, swordlike foliage that is produced freely. Among these arise myriad strong stems that carry the typical brown, fruiting, pokerlike heads during late summer and early autumn. It is these heads that are often dried and used for indoor floral decorations. Height 36–72 inches (90–180cm).

CULTIVATION
Grow in an open, sunny position in either moist soil or up to 12 inches (30cm) of water. A very vigorous plant that requires regular controlling to prevent its fast-growing creeping root system from swamping its neighbors. Propagation is by division during early spring.

TYPHA LAXMANNII

MINIMUM TEMPERATURE **–22°F (–30°C)**
ZONE **4**

CHARACTERISTICS
Strong-growing, hardy, perennial marginal aquatic plant, with tall, upright, narrow, gray-green, straplike foliage. Slender, pale brown, pokerlike fruiting heads are produced during late summer and early autumn. These are sometimes dried and used for indoor decoration. Height 36–60 inches (90–150cm).

CULTIVATION
Grow in an open, sunny position in either moist soil or up to 8 inches (20cm) of water. A vigorous plant that should be carefully observed to ensure that it does not smother any weaker-growing neighbors. Propagation is by division during early spring.

TYPHA MINIMA
(Dwarf reedmace)

MINIMUM TEMPERATURE **–4°F (–20°C)**
ZONE **6**

CHARACTERISTICS
An easygoing, marginal plant for the smaller water feature, especially tub or sink gardens. It is a complete miniature replica of the common reedmace with dark green, grassy foliage and short, chunky, rounded, dark brown seed heads. Unlike its relatives this species is not invasive. Height 18 inches (45cm).

CULTIVATION
Grow in an open, sunny position in moist soil or up to 2 inches (5cm) of water. It will need dividing during early spring every three or four years. Propagation is by division in early spring.

VALLISNERIA SPIRALIS
(Tape grass, Eelgrass)

MINIMUM TEMPERATURE **34°F (1°C)**
ZONE **10**

CHARACTERISTICS
Tropical, submerged aquatic plant forming neat clumps of narrow, tapelike, translucent green leaves. Once established it creeps around, eventually developing into sizable colonies. The flowers are minute and insignificant. It remains evergreen unless the water temperature drops below 41°F (5°C).

CULTIVATION
Grow in up to 12 inches (30cm) of water in a sandy medium in full sun or partial shade. Regularly replace the plants every two years in order to maintain vigor. Propagation is by the division of clumps of plantlets at any time during the growing season.

VERONICA BECCABUNGA
(Brooklime)

MINIMUM TEMPERATURE **–13°F (–25°C)**
ZONE **5**

CHARACTERISTICS
Hardy, semi-evergreen, marginal aquatic plant with scrambling stems that are clothed in dark green, rounded foliage. Dark blue flowers, each with a conspicuous white eye, smother the plant throughout the summer. During most winters the plant remains evergreen, but if the temperature drops below –4°F (–20°C) it is likely to defoliate. Height 6–8 inches (15–20cm).

CULTIVATION
Grow in moist soil or in up to 6 inches (15cm) of water. Makes an ideal plant for disguising the edge of a water feature. Although perennial, much better plants result from regular replacement by short stem cuttings taken during early spring. Propagation is by stem cuttings taken at any time during the growing season, or by lifting and detaching shoots that have rooted in saturated, heavy soil or water.

ZANTEDESCHIA AETHIOPICA
(White arum lily)

MINIMUM TEMPERATURE **32°F (0°C)**
ZONE **10**

CHARACTERISTICS
A striking, perennial marginal plant with handsome, heart-shaped, bright green leaves and white funnel-like spathes, each with a slender central yellow spadix. Dies back during the winter. There are a number of cultivars, among them the slightly smaller and hardier 'Crowborough' and pale-green flowered 'Green Goddess'. Height 24–48 inches (60–120cm).

CULTIVATION
Grow in up to 12 inches (30cm) of water in a greenhouse, outdoors in a warm climate, or as a temporary outdoor inhabitant in cool conditions. When growing in deep water, frost is usually tolerated. Knock waterlily aphids off with a strong stream of water from a hose. Lift and divide every third season, just as the plants start into growth. Propagation is by division and redistribution of the tubers.

ZANTEDESCHIA ELLIOTTIANA
(Yellow arum lily)

MINIMUM TEMPERATURE **34°F (1°C)**
ZONE **10**

CHARACTERISTICS
Wonderful tropical, perennial, marginal aquatic plant with bold, heart-shaped, dark green leaves that are heavily spotted with white. Beautiful bright yellow funnel-like spathes are produced during the summer. Dies back during the winter unless high light intensity and warmth can be maintained. Height 24–32 inches (60–80cm).

CULTIVATION
Grow in up to 8 inches (20cm) of water indoors in tropical conditions, ideally with a consistent temperature of 75°F (24°C). Knock waterlily aphids off with a strong stream of water from a hose. Lift and divide every third season, just as the plants start into growth. Propagation is by division and redistribution of the tubers.

Hardiness Zones

❧

*The temperatures given in these maps
indicate the lowest temperature or range of
temperatures a plant will tolerate.*

Each plant in the Directory
has a number or range of numbers that
corresponds with the zone maps illustrated
here. Once you know what climatic zone
you live in, you can tell at a glance whether
or not a particular plant will thrive in your
garden, or if it needs winter protection.
Remember that hardiness is not
just a question of minimum temperatures.
A plant's ability to survive certain
temperatures is affected by many factors,
such as the amount of shelter given and its
position within your garden.

KEY
Average annual minimum temperature

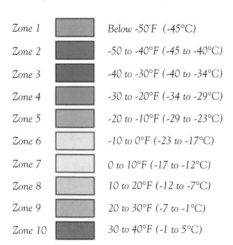

Zone 1		Below -50°F (-45°C)
Zone 2		-50 to -40°F (-45 to -40°C)
Zone 3		-40 to -30°F (-40 to -34°C)
Zone 4		-30 to -20°F (-34 to -29°C)
Zone 5		-20 to -10°F (-29 to -23°C)
Zone 6		-10 to 0°F (-23 to -17°C)
Zone 7		0 to 10°F (-17 to -12°C)
Zone 8		10 to 20°F (-12 to -7°C)
Zone 9		20 to 30°F (-7 to -1°C)
Zone 10		30 to 40°F (-1 to 5°C)

North America

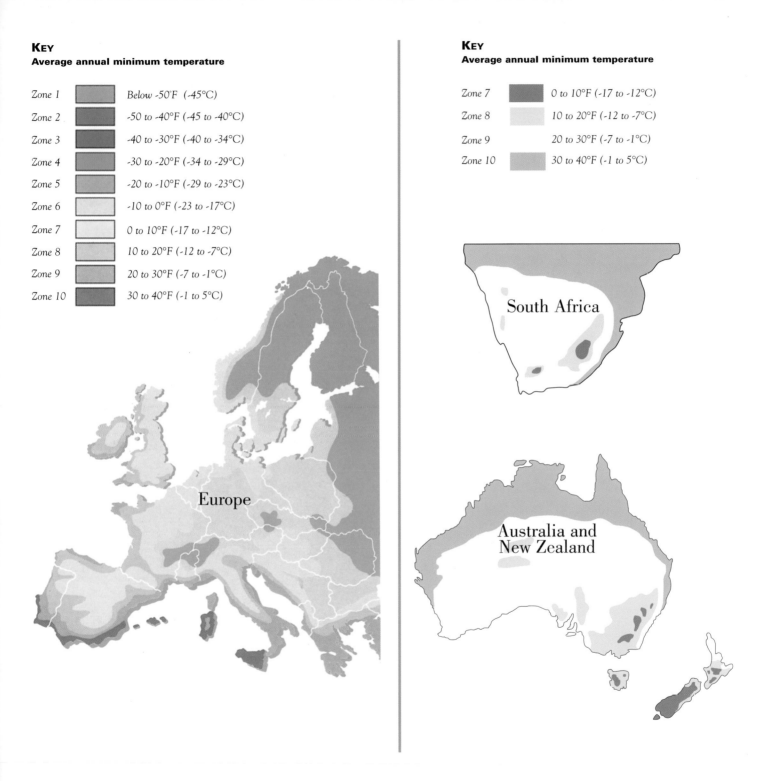

KEY

Average annual minimum temperature

Zone 1   Below -50°F (-45°C)

Zone 2   -50 to -40°F (-45 to -40°C)

Zone 3   -40 to -30°F (-40 to -34°C)

Zone 4   -30 to -20°F (-34 to -29°C)

Zone 5   -20 to -10°F (-29 to -23°C)

Zone 6   -10 to 0°F (-23 to -17°C)

Zone 7   0 to 10°F (-17 to -12°C)

Zone 8   10 to 20°F (-12 to -7°C)

Zone 9   20 to 30°F (-7 to -1°C)

Zone 10   30 to 40°F (-1 to 5°C)

KEY

Average annual minimum temperature

Zone 7   0 to 10°F (-17 to -12°C)

Zone 8   10 to 20°F (-12 to -7°C)

Zone 9   20 to 30°F (-7 to -1°C)

Zone 10   30 to 40°F (-1 to 5°C)

Europe

South Africa

Australia and
New Zealand

Things You Need to Know

❧

General Considerations

Position is everything with a water feature. It is essential that you choose an open, sunny spot and preferably one that is sheltered. Full sunlight is essential for the successful growth of most aquatic plants. It is particularly important in ensuring that plants like irises and waterlilies, which are grown for their flowers, bloom well, and for the longest possible period. You should keep your water feature well away from trees, as they shed troublesome leaves.

Shelter is necessary in order to protect plants from damaging cold winds in early spring, and also to reduce evaporation. When moving water is to be a highlight, you should utilize a quiet corner, as strong breezes blow about the water and might spoil the effect. Indoors, ventilation during summer months and some shade, if the pool is in a conservatory, are essential.

If you are planning to use moving water, make sure that a source of electricity to operate the pump, and of fresh water are close by. If

MOVING WATER
A fountain adds so much to a small container, and is quite safe for children.

not available, such an electricity supply should only be installed by a qualified electrician.

Stability is important, especially for taller containers, and where there are young children about, since water is heavy and can easily overbalance an urnlike feature that is not secured to the ground. Nowadays there

are many strong adhesives that are very effective, but remember that if your container is not frostproof you may need to bring it indoors for the winter.

Small water features have much in common with garden pools, but they can never attain the natural balance that is

achieved in a pool. With a traditional garden pool, the plants, fish, and snails interact harmoniously to create a miniature underwater world. In a container or small water feature, this is not possible. The main reason for this is the wide range of temperatures that such a feature experiences. Sudden soaring temperatures, combined with a high level of nutrients, can create a green algal bloom in a matter of hours. Such intense warmth can also lead to oxygen depletion, and the rapid demise of any fish. So, in many containers fish cannot be used. Routine maintenance is, however, much like that for a garden pool, including regular deadheading of plants, removal of algae, and checking for troublesome aphids.

Make sure to select an appropriate growing medium for the plants in your container water garden—garden soil will not do. The potting mix must be able to sustain healthy growth, but at the same time it must not leach nutrients into the water or cause pollution. Use a soil-based medium, preferably one that has been specially formulated for aquatic plants. The potting mix should ideally be heavy, and any organic matter must be well decayed.

The choice of appropriate plants is important, for many aquatic subjects are fast-growing and can become ungainly. Select plants of naturally modest stature so that any cutting back necessary to keep them within bounds is scarcely noticeable. In many cases, the plants need to be of an easygoing disposition, and you must be able to transplant them successfully.

TAKING CARE

Although easy to maintain, a container water feature needs regular attention.

GETTING THE POSITION RIGHT

Make sure that your container is in an open, sunny position, but also close to a convenient supply of fresh water and electricity.

① *Submersible pump*
② *Plastic tubing that supplies water to the upper container from the pump outlet*
③ *End of tubing, fed through ornamental pump*
④ *Buried electricity point feeding pump and optional light*
⑤ *Vertical windbreak*

Pumps and Fountains

Moving water plays an important role in many container water features. Indeed, the reason for having such a small feature is often that it offers an opportunity to have safe moving water in the garden or on the patio.

All you need to produce moving water are a suitable pump and a simple understanding of both flow rates and filtration. You can greatly enhance the clarity of the water by using a filter attached to the pump, although in many cases a simple filter unit will be built into the pump.

Almost all small water features can be served by a submersible pump. These come in a wide range of shapes and sizes, and usually sit in the container underneath the water and recirculate it as a fountain or waterfall. Some pumps require the installation of a separate, buried cable. But there are many low-voltage pumps, and the cable for these can be run on the surface and be disguised by plants. It must, however, be protected by plastic conduit where people are going to walk. For most small water features low-voltage pumps are perfectly adequate. Only if significant

CASCADING FOUNTAIN
The water is the feature here, as conditions are not suitable for plants.

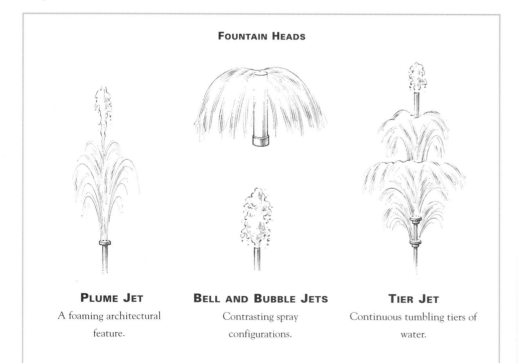

FOUNTAIN HEADS

PLUME JET
A foaming architectural feature.

BELL AND BUBBLE JETS
Contrasting spray configurations.

TIER JET
Continuous tumbling tiers of water.

BELL FOUNTAIN FEATURE
Plants can live happily with gently moving water.

amounts of water are to be moved will you need a more powerful surface pump unit. The provision of the power-supply cable and the method of hiding it are the biggest challenges anyone creating a moving water feature has to contend with.

If you want to construct a straightforward fountain in a sizable, uncluttered container, there is another option. Recently, a small solar-powered fountain has been developed that works without electricity. It consists of a small, round unit with a built-in pump, and a solar panel that is placed on the surface of the water. The height of the fountain jet varies according to the weather, but on a warm, sunny day a jet 12–20 inches (30–50cm) high can be expected.

Whatever configuration of moving water you decide on, it is important to get the flow rate of the water right. When choosing a pump, always select one that will deliver slightly more water over a given time than is required. Having spare capacity allows you to change arrangements if you wish to, and since the pump does not need to work at full capacity all the time, there is no strain on it and its life is extended.

Volume requirements and movements for most small contained features are modest, and calculations based on standard practice may need to be adapted and scaled down. Broadly speaking, in order to assess a pump's capacity for a flowing water feature, pour water over a cascade unit or something similar from a garden hose at the rate desired. Collect the

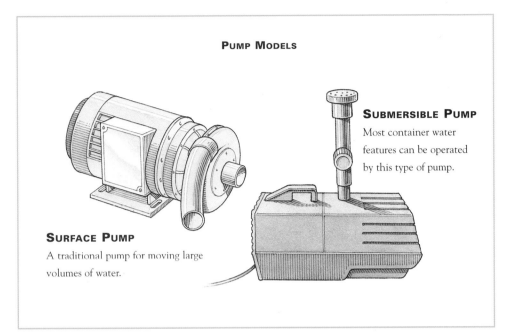

PUMP MODELS

SURFACE PUMP
A traditional pump for moving large volumes of water.

SUBMERSIBLE PUMP
Most container water features can be operated by this type of pump.

water delivered over the period of one minute. Measure the quantity that is collected in quarts (liters), multiply by 60, and you have the number of quarts (liters) per hour that the pump must be able to move to produce the desired result. Potential fountain heights are normally described on the packaging of a pump.

The type of fountain spray created depends on which jet you choose. Jets are detachable and merely push or screw on to the pump outlet. There are many different patterns of spray, and also attachments that will ensure a constantly changing sequence, in the most sophisticated cases synchronizing with lights and music.

MOVING WATER AND PLANTS
This delightful arrangement combines moving water with the happy establishment of plants.

Keeping Water Clear

Small water features are always more difficult to keep clear than large ponds. With a small volume of water, rapid temperature change leads to the growth of algae and oxygen depletion, and in winter it is difficult to sustain a balance of life. Water clarity depends on a balanced environment, which is impossible to achieve in anything less than a modest garden pool.

Unpleasant discoloration of the water, other than from algae, is a different proposition. This is usually a physical manifestation that something has gone badly wrong, such as a dead and rotting fish or plant, or results from neglecting safeguards to prevent the growing medium from spilling or leaching into the water.

In all small water features green water will appear from time to time. The first thing to do to reduce its occurrence is to select your growing medium very carefully. A compost that is high in readily soluble nutrients will create nightmare green conditions, so avoid using ordinary garden compost at all cost. Properly formulated aquatic potting mix contains a minimum of soluble fertilizer, so plants will need regular feeding with tablets or sachets of slow-release fertilizer that is manufactured for

FILAMENTOUS ALGAE
Weeds can completely obscure the water surface.

REMOVING ALGAE
Filamentous algae can only be controlled by hand.

Things You Need to Know **120**

the precise requirements of aquatic plants. If submerged and floating plants are the only aquatics grown, you can use washed pea gravel for the submerged plants, and the container can remain soilless. If one or two fish can be included they will provide sufficient detritus, along with the natural plant detritus, for the nourishment of the plants.

Although it is true that a permanent natural balance cannot be achieved in a small water feature, submerged plants can make some difference. They mop up excess nutrients and therefore prevent algal growth, which helps to keep the water clear.

Without a natural balance, the only reliable way to keep the water clear is by the use of organic algicides. These are particularly effective with suspended algae—some simply kill them, others cause the algae and other organic detritus to form a mat and settle on the floor of the container. The range of algicides available is legion, but make sure to use an organic brand. Provided that the prescribed dosage is adhered to, neither plants, fish, nor snails will suffer.

Filamentous algae present a different problem. They are variously know as silkweed, blanket weed, or flannel weed, and they can only be successfully removed by hand. An organic algicide will kill them, but you still need to remove them in order to prevent them from deoxygenating the water when decomposing. The regular removal of filamentous algae should therefore be part of routine maintenance.

Dirty water resulting from other causes usually means that the feature has to be emptied and cleaned. This is very simple if the death of a fish or plant has caused the

pollution, but it can be a bit more troublesome to prevent soil or compost spillage recurring.

When planted areas or pockets are straightforward, then topdressing the potting mix with a shallow layer of fine pea gravel will prevent soil from escaping into the water, and deter fish from stirring up the soil. When this is not practical, use a piece of old pantyhose, fill it with soil, and mold it to the shape of the planting pocket; the fabric retains all but the finest particles of soil. You

can insert the plants through holes that are just large enough to accommodate them, and the roots will bind the whole package together, preventing spillage.

ALGAE CONTROL

Make sure that your container has fresh and clean water at all times.

Fish and Snails

Fish can be an important component in any water feature, although in some of the smaller types they would not be able to survive a cold winter, or even a warm summer. For the most part, it is the amount of water surface area available that is crucial to the survival of fish. The larger the surface area, the more oxygen is available, although a substantial volume of cool water can also help to sustain animal life. In many containers, irrespective of the surface area available, the violent temperature changes that often occur in a small volume of water make it impractical to introduce fish.

While not essential, fish add considerable visual interest to a small water garden. Although they cannot do much to bring about a natural balance, they are extremely useful in controlling aquatic insect pests, especially mosquito larvae. Where it is not possible to keep fish, a small amount of cooking oil dropped into the water every few weeks is harmless to plants, but prevents the larvae from coming up for air. You can also use mosquito dunks to eliminate these pests.

The dunks release an innocuous chemical into the water that is nevertheless deadly to the active larvae.

If you are able to include fish in your feature, always select small specimens. Fish are remarkable creatures that are able to adapt to their environment by restricting their

CHOOSING FISH

These fish are suitable for container water gardens.

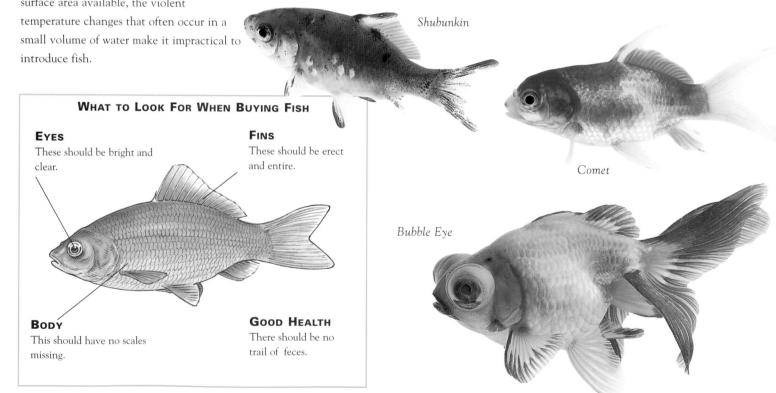

Shubunkin

WHAT TO LOOK FOR WHEN BUYING FISH

EYES
These should be bright and clear.

FINS
These should be erect and entire.

BODY
This should have no scales missing.

GOOD HEALTH
There should be no trail of feces.

Comet

Bubble Eye

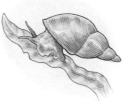
Ordinary Goldfish

Moor

growth to the space available. Thus a small goldfish in a goldfish bowl after four or five years will be much the same size as when it was first introduced, and will be quite healthy and lively. Once placed in a garden pool, the same goldfish will grow very rapidly and can double its size within six months. So it is essential if your fish are to live a healthy life that you use small specimens from the outset.

Not all fish, even small ones, will enjoy or tolerate the constraints of a container water feature. Those with high oxygen requirements, such as golden orfe and silver rudd, will quickly perish. Fancy goldfish,

especially fantails, veiltails, and moors are the perfect complement, as long as they can be given sanctuary during the winter in cold areas. For the most part, a simple unheated aquarium indoors is sufficient to keep them in good condition all through the winter.

When selecting fish it is important to choose those that have bright eyes and erect fins, and appear lively and active (although this is often the result of keeping the fish rather hungry so that they dart about attractively and do not create too much pollution in the dealer's tank). A clean body without any kind of fungal disease and with all scales intact is vital, and there should be no sign of constipation from trailing feces.

Snails can also be introduced to a water feature to some advantage. If you use the ramshorn type, they will keep much of the troublesome filamentous algae under control, especially those clinging to the inside of the container. Ramshorn snails are round, flat, and

disklike, and carry their shells upright on their backs. In very warm conditions they often succumb to the heat, and in heavily populated containers they are sometimes sucked out of their shells by the fish and devoured. Avoid pointed snails or freshwater whelks, which are often sold for water gardens. While it is true that they will eat algae, they will much prefer your prize waterlily.

Fish and snails tend to look after themselves quite well if they have sufficient room and protective plant cover, although in a confined space feeding the fish is useful and fun. Give a good-quality food sparingly three times a week during the summer, never providing more than the fish can clear up in 20 minutes.

RAMSHORN SNAIL

This snail grazes on algae rather than plants.

Calender of Care

Small water features can require almost as much attention as a large garden pool. The time taken to carry out tasks may be much less, but it is just as necessary to be vigilant in ensuring that all is well.

The advice given for fall and winter applies mainly to colder climates.

SPRING

This is the best time to create a contained water feature and to plant it, and to install moving water if you wish to.

Carry out new plantings in existing features and introduce fish where appropriate.

Reintroduce overwintered plants and, where appropriate, divide them. Lift and divide crowded clumps of plants that have remained in the open.

Fertilize established plants, using specially formulated aquatic plant fertilizer tablets, or sachets pushed into the soil next to the plants.

Feed fish if the weather is warm and they are swimming around actively.

SUMMER

There is still time to plant and establish a new water feature. Later plantings do not flower as freely as those made during the spring, but they are still worth your while. Fish can be introduced at any time during the summer months.

Keep a close watch for green and discolored water and use an organic algicide if necessary. You can treat blanketweed and other filamentous algae chemically, but they must still be removed by hand to prevent them from decomposing and deoxygenating the water. As flowering plants fade, remove the old heads and flower stalks. It is not only tidier to do this, but the plants' energy is conserved by preventing them from setting seed. Also remove dead leaves regularly.

Keep an eye open for any pests and diseases. Troublesome aphids are easily dislodged by a strong jet of water.

DEADHEADING
It is important to remove dead heads regularly.

USING FERTILIZER SACHETS

To prevent nutrients escaping into the water and creating a green algal bloom, use sachets of aquatic plant fertilizer. Tear off the protective strip to reveal the perforations and place in the compost next to each plant. Top dress with pea gravel.

FALL

With the approach of fall tidy up all the plants, and remove those that are going to be overwintered indoors from their containers. To overwinter most aquatic plants successfully, plant them close together in deep trays of damp potting mix in a frost-free place. In warmer climates, where the temperature does not drop below 23°F (–5°C), many hardy aquatics are best left where they are to overwinter.

The turions, or overwintering buds, of floating plants such as *Hydrocharis morsus-ranae* (Frogbit) and *Trapa natans* (Water chestnut)—and in the latter case spiky nuts—usually overwinter on the floor of the pool. If you intend to empty the container for the winter, gather a few turions and place them in a bucket of water with a little soil on the bottom. They will keep successfully until the spring. Such tactics are essential if the plants are to be preserved. Even when they would normally be allowed to remain where they are, it is advantageous to be able to start them indoors, particularly if the spring season is late getting under way.

Treat any lingering algae with an organic algicide and, where appropriate, empty the containers, and bring them inside in preparation for the winter.

WINTER

For the small container water garden, winter is not the best time. While it is feasible to retain one or two features, such as a sunken barrel or a lion mask, in good order outside, in general containers are best drained, cleaned, and placed in a frost-free place for the winter.

PREPARING YOUR PLANTS FOR OVER-WINTERING

OVERWINTERING FLOATING PLANTS
Place winter buds in a bucket of water with a little soil on the bottom.

STORING PLANTS
Place the plants closely together in deep trays of potting mix and put in a frost-free place.

Index

Credits

❧

Quarto would like to acknowledge and thank the following for providing pictures reproduced in this book: **The Garden Picture Library**: 6 (John Glover), 7 (Lamontagne), 8 (Ron Sutherland), 9t (John Glover), 10 l & r (John Glover), 11l (Donald Askhan), 12 (Steven Wooster), 13 (Mayer/Le Scanff), 109 (Brian Carter), 110tl (Didier Willery); **Jerry Pavia:** 11r, 92c, 93r; **Harry Smith Collection:** 116, 117, 118 t & b, 119, 120t & b, 121.
Key: r=right, l=left, t=top, b=bottom, c=center

Quarto would also like to thank the following for permission to take location photographs: Anglo-Aquarium Plant Company Ltd, London, UK; London Aquatic Ltd, London, UK; Royal Botanical Gardens, Kew, UK. We would also like to thank the project maker, Ian Howes; and Sally Roth (US) and Frances Hutchison (Australia) for checking the plant directory.

The author would like to thank the following: Jackie Barber, Littlethorpe Nurseries, Ripon, UK; Tropica Aquarium and Water Garden Centre, Moorland Nurseries, Knaresborough, UK; Thirsk Tropical Fish and Water Garden Centre, Thirsk, UK; Oland Plants, Sawley, Ripon, UK.

The index was prepared by Dorothy Frame.